MW00774493

ANATOMY
of a
MOTOR VEHICLE STOP

Essentials of Safe Traffic Enforcement

Joseph Petrocelli and Matthew Petrocelli

43-08 162nd Street
Flushing, NY 11358
www.LooseleafLaw.com
800-647-5547

Quantity Discounts Available

Library of Congress Cataloging-in-Publication Data

Petrocelli, Joseph.
  Anatomy of a motor vehicle stop : essentials of safe traffic enforcement / Joseph Petrocelli and Matthew Petrocelli.
    p. cm.
  Includes bibliographical references and index.
  ISBN 1-932777-24-5 (alk. paper)
  1. Traffic police--United States. 2. Traffic violations--United States. 3. Police patrol--United States--Safety measures. I. Petrocelli, Matthew. II. Title.
HV8079.5.P47 2006
363.2'332--dc22

                                                            2005026375

Cover by: *Sans Serif, Inc.* Saline, Michigan

Table of Contents

Dedication

This book is dedicated to all those who have loved and supported me throughout all my efforts. My mother, Marie Immaculate, who was loving me before I was born; My brothers, Matthew and Russell who have loved me all my life; My wife Carla who shows me what love is every day and our son Luke who is the greatest blessing in our lives. Also, I need to thank my professional mentor, Trooper Ric Ocetnik #3131, of the New Jersey State Police who gave me the proper tactical and mental foundation needed to survive in law enforcement.

Joseph Petrocelli

This effort is dedicated to all my family and friends, especially my wife, Trish, and my sons, Joseph and Nicholas, who are a constant source of love and joy in my life.

Matthew Petrocelli

i

Acknowledgments

We would like to express our gratitude to:

The Passaic County (NJ) Board of Chosen Freeholders and Sheriff Jerry Speziale for allowing us to use departmental personnel, image and equipment.

The Officer Down Memorial Page (www.odmp.org) for permission to use their website information.

Calibrepress.com for permission to reprint one of their articles.

The Jersey Journal for permission to reprint one of their articles.

Geoffrey Tischman Photography (www.gmt-photo.com) for providing expertise in the photography used in this book.

Justin Church for providing graphic arts support.

The individuals shown above for volunteering their time and expertise in preparing this text:

John Pierson	Michael Tucker
Eli Rivera	Carla Petrocelli
George Rosenthal	Russell Petrocelli
Anthony Abate	Not pictured: Carl Padula

Joseph Petrocelli is a Detective with the Passaic County (NJ) Sheriff's Department. He has been with the Sheriff's Department for the last 15 years, after spending 3 years as a New Jersey State Trooper. He is currently assigned to the Motorcycle Patrol Division and serves as the patrol division's Training Coordinator. Det. Petrocelli has been decorated for life-saving, bravery, proactive patrol and his efforts at the World Trade Center immediately after the attacks on 9/11. Det. Petrocelli has earned a Bachelor's Degree in Theatre Arts from Rutgers University, a Masters Degree in Education Administration and Supervision from Seton Hall University and a Masters Degree in Criminal Justice from Rutgers University. He is currently an Adjunct Professor at Passaic County Community College (NJ) and Caldwell College (NJ). He is the founder and lead instructor of SAFECOPS.com, a law enforcement training and consulting company. He can be contacted at:
joepetro2003@hotmail.com

Matthew Petrocelli is an Assistant Professor of Criminal Justice Studies at Southern Illinois University, Edwardsville. His academic credentials include a Bachelor of Science from the United States Military Academy (West Point), a Masters of Criminal Justice from the Graduate School of Public Affairs at the University of Colorado (Denver) and a Ph.D. in Justice Studies from Arizona State University. A former Army officer and Airborne Ranger, his research interests revolve around law enforcement and the police subculture, and he has published articles on use of force and racial profiling. His most recent publications have appeared in *Police Quarterly* and the *Journal of Criminal Justice*.

The authors are brothers who grew up together in northern New Jersey.

The motor vehicle stop is one of the most common and potentially dangerous situations a law enforcement officer can face. There is no such thing as a "routine" motor vehicle stop. An officer can never know the motivations and intentions of vehicle occupants. Officers must continually learn, train on and implement strategies and tactics to ensure their safety.

Of equal importance is the officer's protection of citizens' rights. As a publicly elected Sheriff I know the public demands security but not at the expense of personal liberties. Officers must be trained to be proactive in detecting crime while preserving this nation's most valuable law enforcement asset—The United States Constitution.

The Anatomy of a Motor Vehicle Stop: Essentials of Safe Traffic Enforcement will help officers achieve these objectives. This book takes the officer through the entire spectrum of legal and tactical variables that can influence the outcome of a motor vehicle stop. It will greatly assist any law enforcement officer in terms of technique and safety. Not only does it review specific tactics, it covers crucial peripheral topics such as pre-patrol preparation, discretion and racial profiling.

This book is intended for the police practitioner, police instructor or a student of criminal justice. It provides methods and practices that will help ensure officer safety; real life examples (in the form of "Reality Checks") illustrate the very real danger of this common law enforcement practice. This text is also unique in that it contains written and practical exercises that ensure the reader has learned the material. I believe this book would be an excellent text for any police academy or community college curriculum, as well as an essential addition to the library of any veteran officer.

The lead author is an officer whom I have worked with for six years and has been under my command for three years. I have watched him conduct himself with professionalism and at a high level of competence. I cannot think of anyone I would rather have writing a book about motor vehicle stops. I urge my fellow law enforcement officers to read, digest and discuss the material in this book. In my opinion, it is one of the best and most complete texts on the topic of safe motor vehicle enforcement. You may not agree with all the information, but you will certainly learn.

Sheriff Jerry Speziale
Passaic County (NJ) Sheriff's Department

The goal of this book is exactly the same as the goal of every other book written about police work. It should be the same goal every officer has no matter what he is doing. The goal is to get home safely.

Police work is different than almost every other line of work. In police work you are not allowed one mistake. One mistake and that's it. You're dead. No re-training, no "back to the old drawing board," no "better luck next time," no cut/paste/delete—none of that. You get a Class A funeral, some canned sympathy from the Governor and that's it. You have one chance to do it right. And you have to do it right every single time. It doesn't matter if you worked a double shift or if you are fighting with your wife or if you are sick or tired or hung over. The felon you're dealing with doesn't care. He is going to test you, test you hard and you better win. And to win every encounter, every time, you better be prepared. That's where this book comes in. This book will lay out strategies to help you prepare to win. You will be taught techniques and the theories behind the techniques.

The techniques are simple and they are explained in a simple way. You can read about them tonight and use them on patrol tomorrow. The theories are universal, rooted in basic survival tactics. By understanding the theories you can apply the techniques to whatever situation you find yourself in. This book will not train you to fight your way up from the bottom of some pile or shoot your way out of a deadly situation. It will train you to position your body, position the suspect and control the scene so these lethal encounters never occur in the first place. The best cure is prevention; the best prevention in police work is to have a solid working plan in place with practiced techniques that fit your abilities, allowing you to control the scene and remain safe. This book presents a solid, functional plan; not for a once-in-a-lifetime shoot-out or for an insane vehicle pursuit, but a plan for that most basic of law enforcement activities: the motor vehicle stop.

Motor vehicle stops are the common denominator of American law enforcement. In cities, suburbs and in the country, in rich and poor neighborhoods and at all hours of the day and night, motor vehicle stops are being conducted. Motor vehicle stops are the most common form of enforcement in our country. Motor vehicle stops are so common that they become routine. Officers lose that "first day on the job" intensity and just do the stops as a matter of habit because they know nothing is ever going to happen. Well, things do happen. Every year officers are injured or killed while doing this most common form of enforcement. This book is designed to help eliminate these injuries and deaths. To that end, this book will take the reader from the earliest stage of a motor vehicle stop through its safe and successful conclusion.

Any motor vehicle stop that does not result in injury or death to an officer should be considered a success. Preparing for this success is the professional and personal responsibility of every officer and every supervisor. The preparation begins before the stop is made or even before the violation is observed. This book will go a long way to help an officer plan for that successful, safe motor vehicle stop.

There is no book that can teach you to be a cop. There is no magazine article, seminar or in-service training that can ever prepare any officer for all the different circumstances he will encounter in a 25 year career. Each situation is different. Each suspect is different. Each officer is different. What can be taught is *how to think like a cop*. Once an officer begins to think like a cop he can cut through the differing confusion and chaos each scene presents. Armed with survival-based priorities and tactical positioning the officer will win, no matter what the situation. The officer must arm himself with a specialized thought process, honed by on-going training and education so he is prepared to think each situation through to its safe conclusion. Failure to do so may result in serious consequences. Very real consequences. That is why this book has "reality checks" interspersed in the text. The reality checks are synopses of officers who were injured or deceased while doing this job. The scenarios are not presented to judge the officers or their actions. No one can judge their actions because none of us were there. The deaths are a tragedy and no one can be exactly sure what caused them. But the basic circumstances are known and it would be more of a tragedy if officers did not learn from these situations and history repeated itself. Read the reality checks—not from a standpoint of judging the officer but within the context of the book. Think what you would do to make sure you survive a similar situation.

The theories and tactics presented in this book are designed to help officers survive motor vehicle stops. But the tactics are so universal they can be easily adapted to other law enforcement situations. No matter what type of call it is, an officer can use the techniques outlined in this text. Proper preparation should be a daily routine. The concept of pre-planning a response to an aggressive felon should be common practice. Conducting business in a safe location of your choosing should be used in every situation. Engaging a suspect from a tactical location is not only for motor vehicle stops. Communicating from behind a (non-intrusive) physical barricade is as applicable on a domestic violence call as it is on a motor vehicle stop. The availability of nearby cover and concealment should always be a concern. The use of distance and time are universal, and when properly understood will help an officer on every type of call. Strong, simple verbal commands are taught here but can be used in every situation. Having a backup plan in place and being properly positioned to execute it should always be in an officer's mind. Seemingly minor points like suspect positioning during questioning, the positioning of suspects not being questioned and officer's positioning are actually extremely important on motor vehicle stops and during all investigations.

Every motor vehicle stop is an opportunity. It is an opportunity for an officer to be struck and killed. It is an opportunity for a fleeing felon to injure or kill an officer. It is also an opportunity for a proactive officer to apprehend a fleeing felon. It is an opportunity for an officer to protect his community by neutralizing an aggressive or dangerous driver. It is an opportunity to get an impaired driver off the road. It is an opportunity for an officer to legally stop an individual transporting illegal guns or drugs. The theories and techniques presented in this book will teach an officer to safely and legally contact dangerous motorists.

Hopefully, this book will serve as a foundation for safe traffic enforcement. Officers will read this book and understand the theories. They will implement the techniques and find the ones that work best for them. They will discuss these techniques with others in the field. They will read other books and articles and continually work toward the ultimate goal: serving and protecting the community with active traffic enforcement and always going home safely.

CHAPTER 1

The Basic Unknown-Risk Motor Vehicle Stop

It's 9:01 am and the class *"Motor Vehicle Enforcement"* is about to begin. The instructor introduces himself by name and department. He states how long he has been in the profession and his current assignment. He briefly reviews his career, highlighting schools he has attended and contributions to the profession. He mentions his formal education. He concludes by speaking of his experiences in traffic enforcement and some of the skills and knowledge he has obtained.

Credibility

Why does the instructor use precious class time speaking about himself?

It is to establish his *credibility*. What gives him the right to get in front of a class and speak on this topic? Why should they listen to him? What does he know that they don't know? All these questions should be answered with that brief introduction. The instructor is establishing his base of knowledge and letting the class know they are receiving instruction from a competent, informed, experienced instructor. The instructor should now go further and state the importance of credibility. When the officers are through with the class and on the road they must work to establish credibility as soon as possible: credibility with the person they have stopped, credibility within the community, credibility within the department and credibility in the courts. In most traffic matters that come before the court there is no "hard" evidence—no videos of the offense, no fingerprints, no DNA and no witnesses. It is the word of the officer against the word of the defendant. And in the absence of hard evidence, the judge renders a verdict almost solely based upon credibility. The State always wins the case because of the officer's credibility. It is the officer who has a job with state mandated qualifications; it is the officer who had a background check; it is the officer who is specially trained; it is the officer who has years of experience, it is the officer who has remained topical by reading books and articles about his profession; it is the officer who is impartial; it is the officer who has sworn to uphold an oath. If the officer does not establish credibility with the court, or loses credibility with the court, his career may never recover. This is especially true in a municipal court where an officer may see the same judge week after week for his entire career. If an officer's credibility falls under suspicion one time, the evidence he presents the rest of his career will be viewed as tainted.

Importance of Enforcement of Motor Vehicle Laws

Once the instructor has established the importance of credibility he should endeavor to show the officers the *importance of enforcement of motor vehicle laws*. Ask the students, "Why enforce traffic laws?" Answers will vary from class to class but they should come back to one main point: Ensure the safe flow of pedestrian and vehicular traffic on roadways. More people are injured and killed in automobile accidents than as a result of all other acts under police control (Leonard, 1971). In the United States in 2000 the total economic cost of motor vehicle crashes was $230.6 billion (National Highway Traffic Safety Administration, 2000). Studies have shown that vigorous police enforcement intercepts approximately 1% of street crime; clearly not much of an effect. But police enforcing traffic laws can slow down traffic and have a direct effect on the well-being of many citizens. No matter what type of community the officer is sworn to protect there is a high probability a traffic problem exists. This is due to several factors but basically the population is growing and the roads are not getting any bigger. Most roadways, especially in the east, were paved in the early to middle part of the twentieth century. Back then, there were fewer drivers and cars were mid-sized. In most families only the head of the household held driving privileges. Cars were expensive and a toy for the rich. When the country was paving its roadways it could not foresee multiple-car families and huge SUV's, though that is obviously the norm now. The infrastructure has not grown though the number of drivers and the size of vehicles has.

Consider the damage one driver operating his vehicle illegally can do. Not only is he a danger to himself and his property but he is also a danger to others and their property. And if an accident occurs how many people are affected? How many people are stressed because they are not getting to where they need to be? How many citizens are denied police service because an officer is busy clearing the accident scene and taking the report? How many hourly wages will be lost by workers caught in traffic? Strict enforcement of motor vehicle laws may upset the operator receiving the summons but the other people on the roadway are better off for it.

Officers should understand how many people are affected when a motor vehicle summons is being issued. Obviously the operator receiving the summons is most directly affected, but what about other passing vehicles? At the very least they are happy their local law officer is doing something proactive and not sitting in a donut shop. But more likely, the presence of an officer issuing a summons to a fellow motorist will remind them to slow down. Many people will drive by in each direction in the 10-15 minutes it takes to conduct a motor vehicle stop. That's an awful lot of people slowing down.

The issuing of a summons also allows for a lawful police-citizen interaction. Traffic enforcement is the most visible and most common police-citizen interaction. Most people will never be victims of a felony or be in a situation that requires personal interaction with a professional law officer. The motor vehicle stop is the situation where a citizen is most likely to encounter a law officer. The law officer must make a good impression during the MV stop because that is most likely how that citizen will view all officers and the entire profession. If the officer is sloppy and unprofessional, you can be sure that every time that citizen tells that story he will relish mentioning the officer's shortcomings. On the other hand, if the officer is knowledgeable, fair and professional, that will be the citizen's impression of the entire profession. And the officer should be knowledgeable and professional. There is no reason not to be. The average person may get stopped for MV offenses 2 or 3 times in an entire lifetime. An average officer makes 5-10 MV stops a day. The officer should be in control of the situation. The officer should know what to say and should come across as professional. The officer does this every day. He should be "better" at it then the citizen.

The motor vehicle stop is also an opportunity for a proactive officer to lawfully contact suspicious persons. A well-trained and observant officer will, in some cases, be able to escalate a motor vehicle stop into a criminal arrest. Motor vehicle travel is a common denominator in American society. Every strata of the socio-economic continuum is represented on the roadways, including petty and serious criminal offenders. A motor vehicle stop is an officer's opportunity to legally investigate certain persons and circumstances. The law enforcement profession abounds with stories of "routine" motor vehicle stops leading to the detection of felonies and serious criminal offenders. Proactive enforcement can have a beneficial effect on an officer's career as well as serving the community.

Officer Safety

It cannot be stressed strongly enough or often enough that the most important element of motor vehicle enforcement is *officer safety*. Every thought the officer has, every step he takes, every word he speaks should be after taking into consideration how this action will affect his safety. There is not a motor vehicle violation in this world that is worth injury or death to an officer. Offenders who get away will offend again and can be handled at another time; equipment that is damaged can be replaced. There are always other offenders just around the corner. But the officer must be taught that his safety and well-being is the number one priority in every law enforcement endeavor.

Pre-Patrol Preparation

The officer can take several steps prior to even going out on patrol to ensure he is safe. The officer should have a standard *pre-patrol preparation*. Prior to going out on patrol the officer should ensure his uniform is neat and clean and he has taken the proper personal grooming measures. The officer should review law enforcement supply catalogs from different companies. This will expose the officer to the latest in safety-oriented police gear. The officer should wear comfortable body armor. The officer's shoes should be shined and he should have basic necessary equipment such as a (working) pen and a note pad. You don't want to get up to the offender vehicle then have to borrow a pen and paper to write a name and date of birth. The duty weapon should be clean and functional and less than lethal force weapons should be functional. Expandable batons should be checked monthly. Chemical agents should be replaced yearly to ensure clean deployment and a potent product. The officer should check his magazines and handcuffs and handcuff key. Rubber gloves should be changed often to ensure their integrity. The officer should review the 'hot sheet' to be aware of any stolen vehicles or criminal trends in his sector. He should be attentive at roll call for any changes in procedures and for any safety updates.

Before the tour of duty begins, the officer should perform a safety check of the patrol unit. Initially, the vehicle should be checked for damage. The tour commander should be advised of any existing damage. The officer should ensure all emergency supplies (oxygen, first aid kits, fire extinguisher, flares, life preserver etc.) are present and in good working order. The officer must check the back seat, both the surface and underneath. The officer wants to make sure no objects have been left on the back seat that can be used as weapons. For example, maybe the prior patrol transported a suspect who "offed" a knife by placing it under the back seat while in transit. The prior shift's lazy work ethic should not result in your injury. Other seemingly innocent items can also be weapons in the hands of a motivated offender; a pen can be used like an edged weapon, a flare could be used to choke an officer. The officer must make sure prior to beginning patrol that the back seat is clear of any items and any suspect can be safely and quickly placed there.

The officer should also check the back seat for any contraband. The officer wants to be confident the back seat area is 100% clear of any items prior to a suspect being placed there. The officer can then say with certainty (and under oath) that any items found in the back seat were placed there by the suspect.

The back seat must also be clear of any duty-related items (briefcases, dry cleaning, flares, jackets, etc.). If the officer encounters a violently resisting offender during the tour of duty, the back seat must be clear to allow immediate placement of the individual in the back seat. There may not be time to begin removing items and stowing them in the trunk when a violent confrontation occurs.

The officer should then check the working condition of all automotive equipment. The emergency lights, siren and PA system should be checked. A radio check to dispatch should be conducted. Additionally, the officer's flashlight and portable radio should be checked.

Now that the officer looks good and his vehicle is clean and ready for patrol he must be prepared to perform well. He should take steps to ensure the highest level of competence. The officer should be aware of the stop techniques presented in this and other books—if one technique fails or is not available, the officer should have other techniques in mind. The officer must be up-to-date on the latest legislation and court decisions. Some 20 year veterans still have the same law books they had in the academy. The officer must know if a violation is a primary or secondary violation. The officer should also be aware of the unusual aspects of any law (for example, in the State of New Jersey most people think it is illegal to change lanes without signaling; it is not. It is illegal to change lanes without signaling *only if that movement has an effect on other traffic*). The officer must take steps to understand every aspect of every offense he is sworn to enforce.

The officer should be aware of the statute of limitations for common violations. Prevailing circumstances may preclude an officer from writing a summons at the time the violation occurred. Most jurisdictions give officers (at least) 30 days from the time of offense to take enforcement action. This information is important and should be known prior to going out on patrol.

Though the officer should have a working knowledge of every law, no one would realistically expect him to enforce **every** law **every** time. There is a paradox in law enforcement: People expect strict enforcement of motor vehicle laws, except when it comes to them. The criminal justice system understands that an officer cannot write every offense he sees. Young officers should be made aware that it is okay, rather it is expected, that they do not write every violation they see. No judge, no sheriff, no police chief, no prosecutor and no defense attorney expects an officer to write every violation. The officer is expected to exercise *discretion*.

Discretion

Discretion can be defined as an "exercise of judgment." An officer should be sure to know this definition. Not knowing the definition of discretion led to this testimony in a municipal court:

Defense attorney: "So, do you write a ticket every single time you see this violation?"

Officer: "No, sir."

Defense attorney: "Why not?"

Officer: "I use my discretion, sir."

Defense attorney: "And how do you define discretion?"

Officer: "Well, sir, it is when you have two violations but you only have time…"

Defense attorney: "No, no, no…that is an example of discretion. I just want a definition."

Officer: "umm…well…It's like when you have two people, both speeding…"

Defense attorney: "Again that is an example. I just want a simple definition of a word you used and of something you do everyday…"

And it went from there. The officer squirmed for another couple of minutes and then the case proceeded. Needless to say, this exchange had absolutely nothing to do with the violation and the defendant was found guilty, but it was nonetheless painful to watch. This defense attorney was being childish and grasping at straws but a law officer should know the definition of a common practice like discretion.

Discretion is expected and it is built into the criminal justice system. But improper application of discretion can get an officer, and his department, into a great deal of trouble. Prior to exercising judgment the officer should have some type of decision-making process in place. What factors should an officer consider? What is "good discretion"? The following are some factors an officer should consider:

1) *Severity of the offense.* Severity of the offense and the amount of discretion available to an officer are inversely proportional—that is to say the worse the offense, the less discretion. Obviously the amount of discretion exercised with a vehicular homicide suspect is much less than the amount of

discretion exercised with a speeding suspect. In a motor vehicle offense context the officer should consider the number of people endangered by the offender's action; this would include considering time of day, traffic conditions and the presence of pedestrians. The officer should also consider weather conditions (rain, snow, ice), road conditions and contour (potholes, curves, hills) and other prevailing conditions (work zone, school zone, hospital zone).

2) *Driver's attitude.* Some drivers are truly contrite and realize immediately their mistake. Others want to bicker and question the officer's competence. Still others do not have the time to hang up their cell phone as they provide necessary paperwork. Though the officer does not want to turn the stop into a crying contest, he does want to gauge the operator's remorse. In some cases, when a driver understands the danger he created to himself and others, a warning may suffice.

3) *What else is going on?* The officer must be cognizant of what else is going on in the municipality. For example, if the hospital is burning down, he should not be conducting RADAR enforcement. When responding cross town to a call of Officer Needs Assistance, he obviously should not stop and enforce a cracked windshield violation.

4) *Will the negative outweigh the positive?.* The benefits of proactive motor vehicle enforcement were outlined earlier in this section. But there are times when prevailing negative factors will outweigh the positives. The officer has to be aware of what is going on in the community and where the stop is conducted to minimize the negative factors. For example, 50 outlaw motorcycle gang members are riding through town on a Sunday morning. You are on duty with one other officer. The gang is basically abiding by the laws of the road but cyclist #18 has a cracked taillight. If the officer decides to

stop #18 for this minor violation it is not unfore-
seeable that this could escalate into a major problem. The entire gang will stop. Soon the officer and
his backup will be surrounded, out-numbered and
maybe outgunned. This situation could deteriorate
very quickly and take a long time to rectify. All
this chaos over a broken taillight. Based on the
number of officers working, the number of bikers
and the minor nature of the offense, the officer
should realize the negatives outweigh the positives
in this situation.

5) *Operator explanation.* There are situations where
an operator's personal or professional circumstances may have strongly lent to the driver com-
mitting the offense. Officers should be professional
and somewhat detached but remain compassion-
ate, empathetic and open-minded enough to consider each operator's personal plight.

6) *Departmental policy.* There are times when a department or community is interested in enhanced
enforcement of certain statutes. Based on a large
number of accidents, RADAR enforcement may be
ordered on a stretch of roadway. If a number of
motorists have been hurt in motor vehicle crashes,
seat belt laws may be more strictly enforced. If a
certain intersection is contributing to traffic con-
gestion, red light statutes may be enforced. When
these "crackdowns" are in effect, they will have an
impact on an officer's discretion.

Every situation is unique and other factors may be
present that will weigh into the officer's decision-making
process. But there are some factors that should ***never***
enter the professional officer's thought process. These
factors may be called "bad discretion."

Factors that an officer should not consider:

1) *Race*
2) *Color*
3) *Creed*

   4)   Religion
   5)   Gender
   6)   Sexual orientation
   7)   Handicap

These are factors over which a person has no control. It is illegal, immoral, unprofessional and just plain wrong for an officer to consider these factors. Communities across America are sickened by officers who use these factors as criteria for issuing tickets, and most jurisdictions have an apparatus in place to track officers who do so. When those officers are located, they are first counseled, then should be separated from the profession. Using these factors in the decision making process subjugates the very law the officer has sworn to uphold.

Officers must be especially concerned with racial profiling. Racial profiling is the ascribing of criminal behavior to a person based on their race. It was taught to law enforcement personnel as part of the "War on Drugs" in the 1980s but has since been abandoned as a tool because it caused more problems then it solved. It was found that racial profiling wound up alienating the community the police need help from in fighting crime. Using racial profiling is unprofessional and unacceptable and a quick way to get fired from police work.

Racial Profiling

Racial Profiling and Police Work

Two questions officers often ask about racial
   profiling are:
   (1) Do I need to be concerned about it?
   (2) Does it really exist?
The answer to both questions is yes. Whether or not police intentionally target persons because of their race is increasingly being debated by law enforcement officials, civil rights groups, and ordinary citizens. Equally troubling in the eyes of many are

---

aggressive police traffic stop (or stop and frisk) practices that may have a disparate impact on minorities even if they are not intentionally discriminatory. Officers need to be very concerned with racial profiling because eradicating it has become a high priority of federal, state and local governments. Granted, the terrorist attack on 9/11 has diverted some of the attention and immediacy away from the problem of racial profiling, but it is still an issue of national significance. For example, in his first speech to Congress on February 27, 2001, President Bush addressed racial profiling and directed Attorney General John Ashcroft to develop a set of recommendations to end racial profiling by America's police forces. At least 10 states have passed laws requiring law enforcement agencies to begin collecting data on the racial demographics of motorists stopped by the police, and similar legislation has been introduced or is pending in a number of other states. Currently, U.S. Representative John Conyers (D-Michigan) is sponsoring the proposed Traffic Stops Statistical Act that would mandate the collection of race-related traffic stops data by all state and local law enforcement agencies.

Research on racial profiling is still in its relative infancy, but several of the more prominent studies do validate its existence. In December, 1999 the San Jose (CA) Police Department released the results of an analysis that it conducted on traffic stops in San Jose from July through September 1999. In San Jose, Hispanics make up 31% of the population and accounted for 43% of the persons stopped by the police during the study period. Blacks were stopped at slightly higher rates than their population would suggest (4.5% of the population; 7% of persons stopped), whereas Whites (43% of the population; 29% of persons stopped) were under-represented among motorists stopped. Then San Jose Police

Department accounted for the higher stop percentages among Blacks and Hispanics by pointing out that more police officers are assigned on a per capita basis to minority areas of the city (because of a greater volume of calls for service) as compared with predominantly White areas of the city (San Jose Police Department, 1999).

In one of the largest and most sophisticated studies of racial profiling to date, the New York Attorney General's Office (1999) analyzed more than 181,000 field interrogation cards completed by NYPD officers from 1998 to 1999 and found that although Blacks comprised only 25.6 percent of New York City's population, they accounted for 50.6 percent of all persons stopped by the NYPD. Hispanics were also over-represented among persons stopped, while Whites were significantly underrepresented. Even after controlling for the differential rates at which minorities commit criminal offenses within precincts (as measure by arrests), Blacks (23 percent more) and Hispanics (39 percent more) were still stopped more frequently than White across all crime categories.

As a result of litigation over the allegedly discriminatory traffic stop practices of New Jersey State Troopers, the State of New Jersey undertook a study of stop and search activities of troopers in two state police districts. Examining the stops that occurred from April 1997 through February 1999, and including most of 1996 and a few months from 1994, a New Jersey Attorney General's team found that 627 of the 87,489 traffic stops involved a vehicle search. Of those searches, 77.2% involved Black or Hispanic motorists. During a similar time period, only 33.9% of the total traffic stops made in the two districts were of Blacks and Hispanics (Office of the Attorney General, 1999).

Similar search disparities were found by Lam-

berth (1997) in a study of the stop and search practices of the Maryland and New Jersey State Police.
In a visual survey of traffic violators along the I-95
corridor through Maryland, Lamberth found that
17.5% of the speeding violators were Black, whereas
74.7% of the violators were White. However, of the
823 motorists searched along I-95 from January
1995 through September 1996, 600, or 72.9%, were
Black. In other words, Blacks were being stopped
and searched far more frequently than the rate at
which they were speeding along the interstate. Once
searched, Blacks were no more likely than Whites
to be in possession of contraband.

Likewise, Zingraff et al (2000) analyzed 1998
traffic stop data from the North Carolina Highway
Patrol and found that Blacks were slightly more
likely to be ticketed than Whites when compared to
their percentage among licensed drivers in North
Carolina. Moreover, they found that Blacks were
significantly more likely than Whites to be searched
even though they were slightly less likely than
Whites to be in possession of contraband.

The results from most reported racial profiling
studies indicate that minorities are stopped,
searched and sometimes ticketed at rates that
exceed those for Whites when compared to some
benchmark population (GAO, 2000; Harris, 1999;
Lamberth, 1997; New York Attorney General's
Office, 1999; Office of the Attorney General, 1999;
San Diego Police Department, 2000; Zingraff et al,
2000). Examining individual stops, however, Smith
and Petrocelli (2001) found that although Blacks in
Richmond, VA were stopped at rates that exceeded
their proportion in the driving-eligible population,
they were no more likely to be searched than
Whites and were actually less likely than Whites to
be ticketed or arrested. Moreover, race of the officer
did not predict the race of the motorist stopped, nor

did it predict whether a search or an arrest took place. In a re-analysis of the same data set, Petrocelli et al (2003) explored whether traffic stop, search and arrest practices differed according to racial or socioeconomic factors. They found that: (1) the total number of stops by Richmond Police was determined solely by the crime rate of the neighborhood, (2) the percentage of stops that resulted in a search was determined by the percentage of Black population and (3) when examining the percentage of stops that ended in an arrest/summons, both the percentage of Black population and the area crime rate served to decrease the percentage of police stops that ended in an arrest/summons.

8) *Perceived economic status of offender.* The offender's perceived economic status can affect an officer's thinking two ways—and they are both bad. On the one hand, if the offender is well dressed with nice jewelry in an expensive car the officer may think "he can afford this ticket. I wouldn't usually write this violation but how could it hurt this rich guy?" On the other hand, if the offender is not well dressed and driving an older model, badly weathered vehicle, the officer may think, "I'll just write this guy a ticket. He probably won't pay it anyway. And if he tries to contest it, I'll beat him in court because he's too poor to afford a lawyer." In both cases the officer is wrong for considering the offender's economic status. The summons should be issued on the merits of the offense rather then perceived financial factors.

Officers are wrong for issuing summons based on the above factors. They are just as wrong if they refuse to issue summons based on the above factors (favoritism). If an officer decides his allegiance to a race or nationality or religion or any other factor is stronger then his oath to uphold the law he is guilty of malfeasance. Not writing a summons because "we are all in this together," or "back in the home land they wouldn't approve," is just as wrong as writing a summons based on "bad discretion factors."

Reasons to Stop a Motor Vehicle

With a fair decision-making process firmly in place, the officer will now set out to enforce the motor vehicle laws of his jurisdiction. The first thing the officer should consider is *reasons to stop a motor vehicle.* Based on *Delaware v. Prouse* (1979), an officer must have a lawful reason for stopping a motor vehicle. There are basically four lawful reasons an officer may stop a car:

1) *Motor vehicle offense.* The operator of the vehicle has driven in such a manner or the vehicle is in a condition that violates the motor vehicle statutes of the jurisdiction. The officer has to take special care to make sure the laws he is enforcing have been duly promulgated. That is to say, the law has been enacted and is currently on the books. Just because a sign is posted does not necessarily mean the law is on the books. Private entities, anxious to reduce liability, may post signs on their property that would seem to indicate an action is against the law; in fact the action in question was never outlawed by the necessary governing body—a sign was merely posted.

"Was this sign lawfully placed by the proper authority after a statute was duly enacted by the governing body?"

This is most commonly observed with "No Parking" signs. A private entity will post a sign such as "Parking for President Only" or "Parking for 15 minutes only." These signs appear to be legitimate but under the scrutiny of the court at a trial it would be revealed the action is not covered by statute. These "advisory" signs are common around malls, construction sites and even around government buildings (including police departments) where parking spots are "reserved" for administrative officials.

2) *B.O.L.O.* The vehicle or its operator is wanted in connection with or for the investigation of a criminal justice matter. The officer has been advised to "be on the look out (BOLO)" for the vehicle and/or its operator. When located, the vehicle will be stopped to facilitate the investigation.

3) *Suspected criminal behavior.* The officer comes to know facts which, based on training and experience, would lead a reasonable police officer to believe a specific person has committed a specific crime (probable cause of a criminal offense).

4) *Active warrant.* The officer has knowledge that a warrant is active for the operator and/or a passenger. The vehicle may be stopped to facilitate the arrest.

Exigent or unusual circumstances may arise which necessitate the stopping of a motor vehicle but these are the four main reasons an officer would conduct a motor vehicle stop.

With a fair decision-making process in place, the officer has detected a reason to stop the motor vehicle. For the purposes of this section, we will use a motor vehicle offense for the basis of the stop because that is the most common of the four reasons.

Where to Conduct a Stop

Upon noting the violation and making a determination to stop, the officer should decide *where the stop is to be conducted*. This is an important determination in that the officer's safety, the safety of the violator and the safety of other motorists may be contingent on the choice of location. Certain areas are safe whereas others lend themselves to trouble.

In the case of a high-risk (or felony) stop, the officer should be patient to wait for the safest location. This may take time and may involve leaving his jurisdiction. But he has to be prepared to wait for backup to arrive and for the stop to be conducted in a tactically advantageous area. When backup is in place the officer should think of an area that is away from other traffic and away from citizens. He should also think of areas inhabited by other officers such as the front of headquarters or the front of a jail. These locations are accessible to even more backup. If the front of headquarters or other similar location is not feasible, the officer should think of locations where citizens would not be put at risk. These areas would include industrial parks on the weekends, malls or stadium parking lots during non-business hours or areas around farms. These areas are large and allow the backup officers to get in tactical positions and minimize exposure to non-police personnel.

In the case of an unknown-risk stop, the officer should still be concerned with the location of the stop. The selection of a location for a motor vehicle stop should start much before a violation has been observed. An officer must familiarize himself with his station area. He has to know the flow of traffic and contour of the roadway. He has to know where the roadway narrows and where it broadens. He has to know hills and curves and bridges and driveways and school zones. Only with a complete knowledge of his station area can an officer select the best place to conduct a motor vehicle stop.

An officer should also be aware of *police-friendly* locations and *police-hostile* locations. Police-friendly locations are areas where people with a positive view of the police tend to congregate. These locations would include police stations, firehouses, post offices, houses of worship, town halls, hospitals, construction sites and civic and social clubs. If an officer were to get into trouble it is likely the people at these locations would assist the officer. Police-hostile locations are areas where the police are not generally welcome. Although these areas may not be overtly hostile to police they are areas where caution is required and help should not be expected. These areas include some housing projects, motorcycle club meeting places, certain bars and known gang hangouts. It is up to the officer to determine the police-hostile locations in his station area prior to making a motor vehicle stop or he may find out the hard way.

In choosing the location to stop a vehicle the officer should keep certain ideal locations in mind. These locations should be flat, on a straightaway with good visibility for passing traffic, well-lit with a broad shoulder. A somewhat remote area is better then a congested city street. The area should be accessible to backup officers and a known location to other officers.

Officers should avoid certain locations. The locations to be avoided include:

1) active driveways
2) areas on hills or curves
3) busy intersections
4) bridges (narrow shoulders, very easy for suspect to dispose of evidence)
5) areas with narrow shoulders
6) "radio dead spot" areas
7) any other area where a known danger or distraction is present
8) areas where hazardous road conditions (ice, snow, etc.) are present

Once the location for the stop has been mentally determined by the officer the next thing he has to do is notify dispatch of his intent to stop the vehicle. This is primarily for the safety of the officer. It also allows dispatch to check if the vehicle is stolen or wanted, it makes dispatch aware of the officer's location and makes other officers aware the officer is preparing to conduct a motor vehicle stop. The officer should make every effort to call in the information prior to stopping the offending vehicle. Once the vehicles are at rest, the officer wants to have all pertinent information called in and be prepared to immediately exit the unit.

There are four pieces of information the officer wants to relate to dispatch prior to activating the overhead lights and siren. These are:

1) *Location.* In terms of officer safety this is the most vital piece of information the officer can relay—that's why it is called in first. If something unforeseen happens at least backup officers will know where to proceed to render assistance. When calling in the location, be sure responding officers will be able to find you. This is best accomplished by using large intersections or landmarks. Officer may try to get "cute" and show off their knowledge of the city streets by calling in stops on obscure streets. This is a mistake, as the goal is prompt response from backup, not showing how much the officer knows about geography. The officer should always use cross streets (Main Street at Broadway) instead of street addresses (123 Main Street). On highways or interstates, use the milepost *and* exit number *and* municipality as well as any landmark. Use landmarks whenever possible; What would a Chicago police officer find sooner—1050 West Addison Street or Wrigley Field? It's the same location but one is easier to find.

Reality Check

The Officer Down Memorial Page Remembers…
Police Officer Jennifer Timathy-Ann Fettig

Detroit Police Department, Michigan
End of Watch: Monday, February 16, 2004

Biographical Info
Age: 26
Tour of Duty: 2 1/2 yrs
Badge Number: 128

Incident Details
Cause of Death: Gunfire
Date of Incident: Monday, February 16, 2004
Weapon Used: Handgun; .40 caliber
Suspect Info: Arrested

Officer Fettig and Officer Matthew Bowens were shot and killed while making a traffic stop on Gilbert Avenue at 0200 hours. As the two officers called in the license plate information of the vehicle, while sitting in their patrol car, the suspect exited his vehicle and opened fire with a .40 caliber handgun, striking Officer Fettig several times. The suspect then went out of view as Officer Bowens exited his patrol car and called for assistance. The suspect reappeared and shot Officer Bowens nine times as the officer was taking cover behind his patrol car. Neither officer had an opportunity to return fire. The suspect fired a total of 22 rounds at the officers during the incident. The suspect fled in his pickup truck, but a portion of the shooting was recorded in the patrol car's camera. The suspect and his brother were arrested several hours later. Both officers were transported to Henry Ford Hospital where Officer Bowens was pronounced dead. Officer Fettig was admitted in extremely critical condition and died from her wounds 12 hours later. Officer Fettig had served with the Detroit Police Department for 2.5 years and was assigned to the 4th Precinct. She is survived by her parents and sister.
  Related Line of Duty Deaths:
Police Officer Matthew Bowens
Detroit Police Department, MI
EOW: Monday, February 16, 2004
Cause of Death: Gunfire

2) *Vehicle Registration.* After advising of location, the officer should call in the vehicle's registration. Utilizing the phonetic alphabet, the officer should call in the numbers and letters, then State displayed on the license plate. Officers should be provided with a copy of the phonetic alphabet in the academy and be encouraged to practice as often as possible. Practice can occur as an officer is driving around (on or off duty); by looking at the license plates around him and mentally "calling in" each plate. When the time comes, the officer will be prepared. Whenever an officer prepares to make a stop he is nervous; knowing the phonetic alphabet is one less thing he should have to worry about if he practices beforehand.

3) *Vehicle characteristics.* The officer should advise dispatch of the make, model, color and body style of the offending vehicle. Any other distinguishing factors such as a convertible top, broken or missing equipment and/or bumper stickers should also be called in.

4) *Occupants.* The officer should call in the number of occupants, their perceived genders and race and any other distinguishing characteristics. Some officers are hesitant to call in an occupant's race feeling it will expose him to charges of racial profiling. The information being relayed to dispatch is for the officer's safety; an individual's race is as objective as gender, hair color or color of a vehicle. Mentioning an individual's race is not profiling— ascribing criminal behavior to a person based on their race is.

5) *Nature of offense (optional).* The officer may want to advise dispatch of the nature of the violation. This is generally not necessary for minor motor vehicle offenses but it is essential if the officer senses a heightened level of

threat. Dispatch should be advised of any felony stop, any stop emanating from a drug transaction or any other circumstance the officer feels puts him at risk. Other officers on patrol should be attuned to the nature of the stop a fellow officer is initiating. They may be able to start to the area prior to being advised by dispatch or prior to backup being requested. The time saved will equate to precious seconds in a high risk situation and fosters a culture of professional concern.

An officer preparing to make a stop will be nervous, especially at the beginning of his career. When he first prepares to speak into the radio the nervousness will mount. But the above items must be called in to ensure officer safety. The items above are listed in the order of priority and in the order they should be called in. A simple way for an officer to remember all the information that needs to be relayed to dispatch is to just start at the ground and begin to look up:

When he looks down, he will see the ground—his location – *call it in*.
As he looks up the next thing he will see is the vehicle registration – *call it in*
As he looks a little further up he will see the vehicle make/model/color etc. – *call it in*
As he looks up and through the back window he will see the occupants – *call them in*

By starting at the ground and slowly looking up the officer will systematically and completely advise dispatch of all information pertinent to the stop.

At this point it may be a good time to review proper radio procedures. As part of training, officers should spend some time in dispatch to see how chaotic it can get. Officers have to realize that dispatchers are often multi-tasking, answering phones, checking on phone numbers, handling officers calling in sick, checking information on computers and any number of other activities. Dispatchers are not sitting at the radio, pen in hand, breathlessly awaiting an officer to call in a stop. This being known, the officer has to get the dispatcher's attention before relaying any important information. It is a good habit to wait for the dispatcher to acknowledge the officer before he starts with the stop information.

A good radio exchange should sound like this:

> *"Unit 123 to dispatch with a MV stop"*

> *"Go to dispatch with your stop Unit 123"*

> *"Unit 123 stopping on Main Street at Broadway, Alpha, Baker, Charlie-1,2,3 out of New Jersey. It's a Ford–red, 4-door operated by a white male with a black female front passenger"*

> *"Received Unit 123..."*

The officer should wait for dispatch to check the registration for wants and warrants prior to activating emergency lights and siren.

Once dispatch has advised the offending vehicle shows no wants or warrants the officer should activate the patrol unit's overhead lights and siren. To get the offender to stop where the officer wants, the officer must calculate speed of travel, offender's reaction time and flow of traffic. This is obviously not an exact science but with practice the officer will get the offender to stop where he wants. If the offender does not stop at the location the officer called in the stop, the officer must advise dispatch prior to exiting the vehicle.

The officer should activate the emergency lights and siren on all stops. Sirens are oftentimes not heard by the offender due to rolled up windows, conversations, cell phone calls, radios and air conditioners. The siren should still be activated because it will alert other vehicles, bicyclists and pedestrians of your intent to stop the vehicle and allow these individuals to clear the area. Also, several State laws articulate a driver can only elude an officer who had activated emergency lights *and* siren.

The patrol unit should be at least 3-5 car lengths behind the offending vehicle (depending on speed). If the patrol unit is any further back the suspect vehicle may have time to turn a corner or in some other way elude the officer. If the patrol vehicle is too close the offending operator may not be able to see the wig-wag lights or overhead lights. The officer wants to be far enough back so that the offender can see the entire profile of the patrol unit.

Officers should also be prepared for a sudden response from the operator. Offending operators may become nervous and slam on the brakes. Officers have to be far enough back to be able to react. Operators may stop in the roadway or in the left lane. The officer must safely move the operator to the right shoulder using the unit's PA and/or hand gestures.

After the offending vehicle is aware of the officer and starts to move to the right curb, the officer should place his unit somewhat to the right of the offending vehicle (approximately 1/3 of a car's width); this way, the marked patrol unit will act as an "escort" safely allowing the offending vehicle to proceed to the right curb. It also provides the officer with a better view of the operator, looking through the center of the back windshield instead of directly behind the operator.

As the offending vehicle slows to a stop along the right curb, the patrol unit should drop back. When the offending vehicle is at complete rest, the officer wants to position the patrol unit approximately 10 feet back and 3 feet to the left. The "10 feet back, 3 feet over" is only a guide. For practical purposes, the patrol car should be far enough back so that the officer can see the offending vehicle's rear tires on the road and aligned to the left to the point where the unit's right headlight is directly behind the offending vehicle's license plate. The front tires should be cut to the left, giving on-coming traffic a visual guide and physical channelization to move to the left. The turned front tires also may provide slightly more cover from ricocheting bullets. The vehicle should not be directly behind the offending vehicle because some knowledgeable offenders know if they back up hard enough into the front of the unit, the air bag will deploy allowing for an escape.

Exiting the Patrol Unit

With the offending vehicle and patrol unit at complete rest, the officer must prepare to *exit the patrol unit*. Care should be taken in exiting the vehicle because "each year more officers are injured or killed by accident than are injured or killed by hostile circumstances during a motor vehicle stop" (Connor, Mitchell and Standen, 2000). Prior to coming to complete rest, the officer should have already:

1) removed his seatbelt, extinguished any cigarette, set down any coffee and removed any toothpicks.
2) unlocked all doors and rolled down at least one front window (the front windows allow possible emergency entrance to the patrol vehicle but more likely are insurance against the unit's automatic door locks locking the officer out of the unit).
3) turned on the portable radio
4) have a method of non-lethal force available. If a situation arises where deadly force is required, supervisors, investigators and the courts will

     expect that non-lethal force was available as an option to deadly force.

5)   have a flashlight available, no matter what time of day. This will assist in vehicle searches or in a foot pursuit into a dark business or house. (Rayburn, 2002).

The officer should be ready to exit his unit immediately upon the vehicles coming to rest. After a good look back to check on approaching traffic, the exit should be done very quickly and with an almost constant eye on the occupants of the offending vehicle.

Approaching the Vehicle

The officer must now decide how to *approach the vehicle*. As previously stated, the officer's safety is the number one priority at all times. Much has been said and written about the right way to approach an offending vehicle when there is, in fact, no "right" way. The right way is the way each individual officer is most comfortable with and the way the officer feels affords him the most safety. The right way is the way an officer can safely and efficiently achieve his law enforcement goals. Traditionally, officers have approached on the driver's side. In most movies and on most television programs the stop is conducted on the driver's side. Most people who have been stopped have been approached on the driver's side. Motorists have come to expect an approach from the driver's side. It is for this reason, and several others, it is recommended the officer approach on the *passenger side*.

Positive aspects of an approach from the passenger side:

1)   *Element of surprise.* As stated, most motorists expect a driver's side approach. Approaching on the passenger side adds an element of surprise to the stop in favor of the officer.

Reality Check

Trooper Frederick Anthony Hardy

Michigan State Police
Michigan
End of Watch: Saturday, November 6, 1999

Biographical Info
Age: 36
Tour of Duty: 9 yr
Badge Number: Not available

Incident Details
Cause of Death: Struck by vehicle
Date of Incident: Saturday, November 6, 1999
Weapon Used: Automobile
Suspect Info: Sentenced to 15 years in prison

Trooper Hardy was killed after being struck by another vehicle on I-96 in the Detroit area. Trooper Hardy was exiting his cruiser during a traffic stop, when another vehicle struck him, killing him instantly. The suspect vehicle then fled the scene. However, the suspect was arrested in the following days. He was later convicted of manslaughter and sentenced to 15 years in prison.

Trooper Hardy had been with the Michigan State Police for nine years and is survived by his wife and two children.

2)   *Better view of vehicle interior.* The officer has better view of the vehicle interior. This serves the officer on several levels. 90% of the American population is right-handed. If an offender is holding a weapon it will most likely be in his right hand. The officer will have a much clearer view of the offender's right hand from the right side of the vehicle. It would be impossible for an offender to use body positioning to obstruct an officer's view of his right hand. With practice in using the offending vehicle's right exterior rear view mirror (which most vehicles are equipped with) the approaching officer will be able to see the offender's right hand from a position next to the right rear quarter panel area.

Officers should also be aware that a right-handed shooter would not have to turn and shoot across his body with a right side approach. An offender could get off a good shot with his hand in the area of the front passenger head rest or seat back. The officer has to be very cognizant of this fact on his initial approach.

A right-handed offender expecting a driver's side approach would most likely attempt to conceal contraband in his right hand. Anticipating a driver's side approach, vehicle operators can attempt to conceal contraband with their right hand in the center console, in the glove box or on the front seat. They then attempt to use body positioning to obstruct an officer's view. A passenger side approach would negate this tactic.

A passenger side approach allows the officer a greater square foot plain view search of the vehicle interior. The entire passenger area is accessible for a plain view. It is very common that offenders retrieve required paperwork from the glove box, center console or visor. The passenger side approach affords a better view of all these areas as well as ashtrays and interior compartments. Most right-handed males keep their wallets in their right rear pants pocket. By being on the passenger side, the officer has a clearer view of this side. A female almost always has her wallet in her pocketbook, with the pocketbook resting on the front passenger seat. When opened to remove the wallet, the officer has a clearer view of the contents.

A passenger side approach also allows a better plain scent search. Any contraband that has been smoked is likely to be in the ashtray. The officer has a better view and a better chance of smelling any items in the ashtray. Also, the wind from passing traffic is not as distracting on the passenger side.

View of vehicle interior from left door jamb. *View of vehicle interior from right door jamb.*

The officer on the passenger side has to crouch down much less than an officer on the driver's side to see the operator's hands and vehicle interior. If the stop is conducted on a street where a curb is present, the officer can stand on the curb, allowing him a better (higher) vantage point into the vehicle.

A passenger side approach allows a better view of the vehicle's ignition to ensure it has not been tampered with, as is the case with many stolen vehicles. The officer has a better view of the gear shift and can be aware if the operator inadvertently left the vehicle in "drive."

3) *Distance.* A passenger side approach allows an officer to keep his distance from an unknown operator. Distance is always an officer's friend in approaching an unknown situation. The passenger side approach allows the officer to conduct the stop out of the reach of the operator. If an offender is hostile or aggressive, the distance provided by a passenger side stop will serve an officer well. A motivated offender who wants to grab and drag an officer would be unable to do so if the officer uses a passenger side approach. An officer is much safer from physical attacks as well as attacks from knives and chemical weapons.

On the driver's side a push, opening door and maliciously driven offender vehicle could force the officer into traffic.

If an officer decides to order an operator out of the car, when the operator exits, the officer has the time and distance provided by the hood to observe the operator in a standing position.

REALITY CHECK

Bayonne cop dragged 6 blocks by fleeing driver
By Ronald Leir
Reprinted with the permission of the Jersey Journal

A Bayonne (NJ) police officer escaped serious injury yesterday after police say a motorist she stopped for a traffic check suddenly pulled her halfway into the car and drove off with her holding on for roughly six blocks on one of the county's busiest roadways.

Luckily, an off-duty Jersey City police detective who happened to be driving in the area gave chase, shot at the car and got the driver to stop and both officers grabbed him.

The female officer suffered what police described as relatively minor injuries.

Police Director Mark Smith said the episode began at 7:07AM as Officer Kimberly Kay, 35, a four-year member of the force, was on patrol duty in the city's uptown area when a 1993 four-door blue Honda traveling north on Kennedy Boulevard near Marist High at 57th Street caught her eye.

The car had an expired inspection sticker, Smith said.

Kay ordered the driver, an Hispanic man in his mid-30's, to pull to the curb, which he did, Smith said, and the officer asked for his paperwork, which the driver fumbled around for but couldn't produce.

Smith said Kay, who had initially radioed in her motor vehicle stop to headquarters, now began calling for a backup unit.

As Kay was in the process of calling in, Smith said, the driver allegedly reached through his fully open window, grabbed the officer, pulled her halfway into his car with her legs dangling outside and floored the accelerator and pulled away from the curb, in the process striking a northbound car waiting at a red light at the 57th Street Intersection.

Smith said the driver then backed up and sped away northbound on Kennedy Boulevard, deliberately guiding his car into the concrete median barrier separating northbound and southbound traffic as he approached the Jersey City border, just past Mercer Park, trying to dislodge the officer, to no avail.

All the while, Smith said, Kay continued to struggle with the driver, trying to gain control of the wheel or the gear shift to bring the car to a stop.

Because of the way she was wedged into the car, Smith said, the officer was unable to reach back for her weapon.

"As the operator exits, the offending vehicle provides a buffer between the officer and the operator and traffic."

4) Avoiding Traffic. A passenger side approach minimizes the risk from passing vehicles. Every year officers are struck by passing vehicles causing injury or death. An officer on a motor vehicle stop should be concentrating all his energies on the offending vehicle. With a driver's side stop, the officer has to be concerned with passing traffic.

On night stops, an officer can make himself more visible to passing traffic by wearing an outermost garment that has some reflective material. Major police suppliers are making jackets with reflective material along the sleeves and/or back. These jackets do not in any way impede the officer's motion but make him more visible to passing traffic. In extreme cases (extremely dark, rural or winding roads), an officer can wear a traffic vest during his tour of duty. A traffic vest should be worn at all times during an accident investigation.

5)   *Facilitates locating cover and concealment.* If a stop deteriorates to the point the officer has to seek cover, the passenger side will allow the officer to locate cover more quickly and safely. From the driver's side an officer is limited as to which way he can run if he is seeking cover. He cannot run forward because he will be in the path of travel of the vehicle or in the sights of an aggressive offender. He cannot run to the right because the offending vehicle is there. He cannot run to the left because of oncoming traffic—he can only run one way—back toward his vehicle. From the passenger side the offender can run back to the unit, run to his right or run forward angling to the right. In an urban setting running to the right or to an angle front and right will allow access to a business or other establishment. In a rural setting, trees and other foliage would provide cover and concealment. In a residential setting, houses or parked cars would be present. In all cases, a curb or guide rail would be present to impede an offender from driving toward the officer.

The officer is too close to the operator and oncoming traffic as the operator exits the vehicle.

Reality Check

The Officer Down Memorial Page Remembers…

Police Officer Gary Neil Priess

DeWitt Township Police Department
Michigan
End of Watch: Tuesday, January 25, 2000

Biographical Info
Age: 43
Tour of Duty: 18 yrs
Badge Number: Not available

Incident Details
Cause of Death: Struck by vehicle
Date of Incident: Tuesday, January 25, 2000
Weapon Used: Automobile; Commercial
Suspect Info: Guilty of negligent homicide

Officer Priess was killed when he was struck by a tractor trailer while making a traffic stop on U.S. Highway 27 near the I-69 interchange. Officer Priess was speaking with the driver of the vehicle he had stopped, when the tractor trailer struck his cruiser, and then him. The driver of the tractor trailer pled guilty to negligent homicide and was sentenced to 90 days in jail, 2 years probation, and 60 hours of community service.

Officer Priess is survived by his wife and two young children.

Reality Check

The Officer Down Memorial Page Remembers...

Corporal Matthew Thompson

Mobile Police Department
Alabama
End of Watch: Thursday, February 12, 2004

Biographical Info
Age: 43
Tour of Duty: 18 yrs
Badge Number: Not available

Incident Details
Cause of Death: Struck by vehicle
Date of Incident: Wednesday, February 11, 2004
Weapon Used: Not available
Suspect Info: Not available

Corporal Thompson succumbed to injuries sustained the previous day when he was struck by a vehicle while working the scene of an accident on Spring Hill Avenue. He was assisting with putting one of the other cars onto a wrecker when he was struck by another car in the dark, rainy conditions. Corporal Thompson was not wearing a reflective traffic vest at the time. He was transported to University of South Alabama Medical Center where he succumbed to his injuries the following day. Corporal Thompson had served with the Mobile Police Department for 18 years. He is survived by his wife, son, and two daughters.

6) *Operator may open the passenger door.* When an officer approaches on the passenger side, he should knock on the window at the point where it meets the door. At the very least the offender will lower the window, but the offender may open the door. By reaching across the passenger seat and opening the door the officer has a clear view of the offender's opened right hand. With the door open, the officer now has a greater sight and smell of the vehicle interior. Initially, the offender cannot be ordered to open the door but if he does so voluntarily, it is legal.

7) *Avoiding a fleeing vehicle.* An offender who decides to flee the scene after stopping will have to pull to the left to enter traffic. For this reason the officer is safer on the right side of the vehicle.

Negative aspects of a passenger side approach:

1) *Walking between the vehicles.* This is generally stated as the greatest detrimental factor of approaching on the passenger side. The officer approaching on the passenger side has to walk in front of the unit and behind the suspect vehicle. It is said that a motivated offender could back into the officer causing serious injury or death. This is no doubt the case; if an offender is vicious and murderous enough, he could back into an officer as the officer walks between the vehicles. But this presupposes the offender is anticipating the officer's path. As previously stated, most operators plan for and are expecting a driver's side approach. The element of surprise should negate this attack by the offender. But for the sake of argument, let's say it doesn't. The offender would have to see the officer make the right turn and begin to walk between the cars. At that time the offender would have to put his vehicle in "re-

verse," wait for the gear to catch, then accelerate in reverse to strike the officer. An officer moving briskly (as he should) on a motor vehicle stop will be between the cars for approximately one to three seconds; is this enough time for an offender to commit this felonious act? Probably not.

Before walking behind the offending vehicle the officer may ensure the vehicle is not in "Reverse."

The offender may have the car in reverse gear, waiting for the officer. The officer must be attuned to this fact and not walk between the vehicles if the offending vehicle is in reverse gear (denoted by the presence of the reverse lights being on).

An officer walking between the unit and the offending vehicle must be cognizant of many things: How long did it take the vehicle to stop? What gear is the vehicle in? Are the operator's hands on the steering wheel? Are they on the gear shifter? Are the hands visible? Is the offender watching the officer?

An officer must remember that just because he approaches on the driver's side does not mean the threat of being backed over has been eliminated. If an offender wants to back over an officer all he would have to do is wait for the officer to get even with the back seat then pull forward about 10 feet to back over the officer. This is something an offender anticipating a driver's side stop may plan. An offender could also grab and drag an officer on the driver's side; this is highly unlikely from the passenger side.

2) *The unit is struck by a passing vehicle.* It has been argued that if the patrol unit is struck as the officer is walking between the cars, the officer can be pinned and sustain injury or death. This is a valid argument, but this fact must be weighed against the amount of time an officer would spend on the driver's side conducting the stop. It seems safer to walk between the vehicles for 1-3 seconds (risking a rear end collision) than to conduct a 3-5 minute motor vehicle stop on the left side of the offending vehicle (risking being struck by passing traffic).

3) *Walking behind the unit.* In order to avoid walking between the unit and the offending vehicle, some officers walk behind their vehicle to approach on the passenger side. This is dangerous because the officer cannot keep visual surveillance on the occupants when he is behind his vehicle. Also, in that brief period of time, if there is a rear end collision the officer would absorb the hit directly.

4) *Presence of passengers.* The passengers in a vehicle will be as surprised as the operator with a passenger side approach. The officer must take special care to make sure the passenger's hands are visible. A passenger may use body positioning to obstruct the vehicle interior. Passengers should be given verbal orders to "show your hands;" failure to comply heightens the level of threat. Additionally, male vehicle operators with female passengers may become upset if they perceive the officer's passenger side approach was motivated by factors other than safety. As always, be cautious about reaching across vehicle occupants.

Reality Check

The Officer Down Memorial Page Remembers...

Trooper Rick Lee Johnson

Michigan State Police
Michigan
End of Watch: Saturday, May 6, 2000

Biographical Info
Age: 35
Tour of Duty: 5 yrs
Badge Number: Not available

Incident Details
Cause of Death: Struck by vehicle
Date of Incident: Saturday, May 6, 2000
Weapon Used: Automobile
Suspect Info: Injured in accident

Trooper Johnson was killed after being struck by a vehicle during a traffic stop on I-94 in Van Buren County, Michigan. The trooper had approached the vehicle on the passenger side, and was returning to his Chevy Tahoe cruiser when a third vehicle ran off the roadway, and rear-ended his vehicle just as he was walking in between it and the vehicle he had stopped. He was momentarily pinned between the two vehicles before the Tahoe spun into the travel lanes, trapping him underneath. Trooper Johnson was flown to a local hospital where he was pronounced dead. The driver of the vehicle, which struck him, received minor injuries in the crash. On the day before the incident, Trooper Johnson had convinced a suicidal man not to jump off of an overpass near the site of the accident. Trooper Johnson had been with the Michigan State Police for 5 years, and is survived by his wife and young children.

The Initial Point of Offender Contact

The officer approaching on the passenger side should pre-decide where the *initial point of offender contact* will be. Officers want to be in a position which allows them to safely conduct the stop and also be in position to detect and respond to other offenses. Prior to exiting the unit, the officer should assess the amount of other traffic on the roadway. It is worth waiting a few extra seconds to allow other vehicles to pass if it mitigates the threat of being struck by a passing vehicle. Upon exiting the vehicle and approaching the suspect vehicle the officer must have his attention on the occupants. The officer wants to approach the vehicle quickly but does not want to rush in. Only with training and experience can this concept be operationalized.

The officer may want to very briefly delay in the area of the unit's left headlight to ensure nothing is overtly out of the ordinary. The officer would then proceed between the two vehicles, placing his left hand on the offending vehicle's trunk. The placement of the left hand achieves three goals. First, it makes sure the trunk is secure and no one is hiding in there, planning an attack on the officer (though many newer model cars have interior emergency trunk releases which would allow egress from the locked trunk interior, it is still a good habit to check). Second, the officer will leave his palm print and fingerprints on the trunk. In the case of mortal injury and offender escape this will serve investigators well in proving the suspect vehicle was the one the officer had contacted. Third, if the suspect vehicle does feloniously back up, the officer can use the trunk to boost himself above the bumper and land on the trunk or the hood of the unit. The officer should attempt to make contact with the trunk in a manner that would not alert the occupants to his position—do not lose the element of surprise if you don't have to. While checking the trunk, the officer should be looking into the vehicle interior at the occupants while moving quickly between the vehicles with his hand near his weapon.

As the officer comes around the right rear of the vehicle, he should briefly look into the back seat area. The officer should be moving briskly but not so hastily that he can not change directions quickly if a threat is present. At this point of the stop, the officer is looking into the back seat only to check for a person or other obvious threat. He is not conducting a plain view search for contraband—that will come later. The officer must be concerned with persons and their hands at this point. Any evidence in the back seat area will remain inert as long as no one touches it. The officer must be concerned with his safety, not the recognition of evidence. If the back seat is clear, the officer should come around the side of the vehicle and stop when he is about equal with the doorjamb. The officer should be slightly behind the vehicle operator. The officer's body should be in a bladed position with his weapon furthest from the vehicle. The front leg (left leg on a right-handed officer) should be bent. At this time the officer should be prepared for a surprise from the vehicle interior and be in a stance conducive to drawing his weapon or returning to the unit.

Passenger side approach, body bladed, hand near weapon, getting a good view of the vehicle interior without exposing his body.

The officer should be concentrating on the hands of the occupants. The officer does not want to merely see the occupant's hands but rather wants to see the interior of the occupant's hands. If the officer cannot see the contents of the occupant's hands he should provide a clear, simple verbal command—"Open your hands, please." Most occupants readily comply with this order. Failure to comply indicates a heightened risk.

The officer should then knock on the window about where it meets the door. The operator will at least roll down the window but may open the door. Beginning with the operator's hands, then his person, the officer should visually scan the vehicle interior for any suspicious movements, items or circumstances.

In absence of these the officer now proceeds to *securing pertinent paperwork.*

Seeing a suspect's hands means seeing the insides of his hands. A seemingly compliant suspect may be concealing a deadly weapon. BE VIGILANT.

Securing Pertinent Paperwork

Similar to the vehicle approach, different officers secure the paperwork in different ways. And similar to the vehicle approach the "right" way for each officer is the way that works best for him. It is recommended the officer forgoes the introduction (i.e. "I'm Officer X from Anytown Police Dept."); these are basically unnecessary words which do not promote any enforcement goal. This introduction can lead to the offender responding with, "Excuse me?" or "What's your name?" or "What department?" All these facts will be abundantly clear to the operator in a few brief seconds.

The officer should direct the operator to produce a driver's license, vehicle registration and any other paperwork required by law. Some officers advise of the violation then request the paperwork. This tactic often leads to the offender stating his case or arguing with the officer. There may be a time and place for this interaction during the stop but for safety purposes the officer must first obtain the operator's credentials. The offender knows who the officer is, while the officer does not know the offender. The officer must try to reduce the information gap that exists between himself and the offender. In deciding whether he should ask for credentials first or advise of the violation first, the officer should ask himself: *What is more important, you knowing him or him knowing the violation?*

Watch the suspect's hands FIRST!

From a psychological perspective it is best to get the credentials first. At the beginning of the stop the offender has something the officer wants: the credentials. From a safety standpoint and a psychological standpoint the officer is at a position of disadvantage. As long as the operator has something the officer wants, he exercises some type of control over the officer and the situation. It is not a physical control but it is a psychological control. The offender can move ahead stating his case or arguing his point while the officer must wait for the credentials. If the officer insists on seeing the credentials, it is now the offender who has to wait for the officer to state the offense. Most States require operators to produce credentials "on the officer's request." Failure to do so constitutes a heightened threat and a criminal offense.

The officer should not ask the operator for pertinent paperwork; rather, the officer should direct the operator to produce the paperwork. This may seem like a small point of semantics but in the human dynamic that is the motor vehicle stop, it is a major point. If a person is asked to do something, the answer to the request can be "No." But if a person is directed to do something he has no lawful recourse but to comply. By directing, not asking, the officer psychologically asserts his lawful authority and maintains control of the stop.

From the position near the doorjamb the credentials should be received in the support (non-weapon) hand. The credentials should be handed out to the officer. The officer should never reach into the vehicle to accept the credentials. The officer should accept only the required paperwork. If a wallet with a license is presented, have the operator remove the license. The officer does not want his hands hindered by this task nor does he want to be in possession of other personal papers or money at any time. The officer should briefly scan these articles for pertinent information. Once this information has been checked and if there are no questions, the credentials should be stowed in a pocket. The officer does not want to encumber his support hand for the entire stop holding 2 or 3 pieces of paper. The officer may now advise the operator of the reason for the stop. The officer then asks, "Is there any reason you committed this violation?" This question serves two purposes. Most operators seize this opportunity to state their case. As the operator is speaking, the officer should begin to move to the front of the vehicle. While he is moving he must watch the occupant's hands but he also wants to complete a visual scan (plain view search) of the vehicle interior from his changing perspective. He should ultimately wind up near the right support of the front windshield, looking through the windshield into the vehicle.

Once the officer is certain the operator's hands are empty and he has received the credentials, the officer should move forward to facilitate his plain vehicle search of the vehicle interior.

As the offender speaks, the officer should be making mental notes that will ultimately become information used against the offender at trial. For example, if the answer to, "Why were you speeding?" is "I'm late for class," that information should be permanently noted. It will buttress the officer's case should the matter go to court. Most violators will talk their way into trouble before they talk their way out of trouble.

The officer is not only noting the content of the offender's statement but the offender's appearance and demeanor. Is the offender intoxicated or impaired? Is the offender rambling? Is the offender trembling? Is the offender failing to answer simple questions with a simple answer? The officer is gauging the offender's response as a possible indicator of latent criminal activity.

The officer may ask some cursory questions such as, "Where are you coming from?" "How long were you there for?" "Where are you heading?" Extreme nervousness or inability to answer simple questions should heighten the officer's concern about the presence of offenses other than the motor vehicle violation. The officer should practice conducting brief roadside investigations within the context of the motor vehicle stop.

Driver's Reaction to Being Stopped

The officer should have a plan in place for possible *driver's reaction to being stopped*. Thankfully the vast majority of violators are cooperative, polite and contrite. But the officer must be prepared for that rare occasion where the violator has a different reaction. Two other reactions that are common are anger and aggression. The officer should be able to identify the difference and have a plan in place for both.

Anger is an emotion. It is a state of mind. It cannot hurt an officer. It may sound bad and it may look bad but it is not a threat to an officer's well-being. A violator can yell or scream or pout or even mildly threaten and a professional officer should be able to take it and still do his job. An angry violator may sit in his car and scream at the officer. He may threaten to call his lawyer, the officer's supervisor, the mayor or any other cast of characters. He may promise a lawsuit and he promises the officer he will soon "have his badge." But all this is done while seated and seat-belted in his vehicle.

Aggression is an action—it is anger in motion. It is an absolute threat to an officer and his well-being. It is the action that is likely to lead to an officer being injured or killed. Officers must be able to identify aggressive behavior and react before they are injured. Aggression begins when the violator makes a threatening gesture to the officer. Any action the officer can articulate as threatening falls under the category of aggression. Officers must be careful because not all aggressive individuals are necessarily angry. They may be seething, planning their attack quietly. But as the aggressive person approaches, the officer must activate his professional use of force continuum. The officer should have a pre-plan in effect to handle aggressive offenders. De-escalation techniques such as *Verbal Judo* have become popular in the last decade. An officer should try to familiarize himself with these techniques as these skills are becoming the expected level of first response. If a violator exits his vehicle in any manner the officer should take steps to create distance and put a physical barrier between the offender and himself, yet the officer does not want the physical barrier to impede the officer's ability to get to his unit. From a distance, a clear, simple, verbal order should be given for the violator to "stop and return to your vehicle." If the violator continues, the officer should move as quickly as possible back toward his unit as he is giving verbal orders for the offender to desist. The officer should move back to his unit only if he can do so safely and from a position of tactical advantage. An offender closing quickly on an officer may very well eliminate an officer's ability to move safely back toward the unit.

Officer moves toward the cover and concealment of his unit while ordering the operator to "Stop, be seated."

Moving toward the unit will allow the officer to seek cover in the vehicle or leave the area if the situation requires. It will allow the officer to contact dispatch with the (more reliable) unit radio. If there is a physical confrontation the officer wants it to occur away from the offender vehicle and nearer the unit. This will show the court that the officer made efforts to defuse the situation by retreating from the point of initial interaction; it would then be obvious to the court that the officer was pursued by the offender and the offender instigated a physical defensive response from the officer.

Once in the area of the front/center of the unit the officer should assume his ready (fighting) stance and execute another verbal command. If the violator continues to proceed toward the officer (this constitutes physical force) the officer should be ready to respond with mechanical force. It is recommended that mechanical force should be dispensed if the aggressive violator continues to within 4-6 feet of the officer. This distance is selected because that is the manufacturer's recommended distance for the proper application of OC pepper spray. At this point the violator would be placed under arrest and departmental procedures would be followed.

From behind the unit's driver's side door, the officer can safely call for backup and give verbal directions to the non-compliant operator

Issuing a Summons

In most cases the violator will be compliant. The officer has received the credentials, stated the violation and conducted his plain view search (which is negative). The officer has heard the violator's explanation and has decided he will be *issuing a summons*. The officer should advise the violator of what enforcement action he plans to take and clearly state what he expects the driver to do: "Sir, you will be receiving a summons for speeding. Remain in your vehicle."

By telling the offender what is planned the officer allows him to react while the officer is standing in a ready position. It shows the officer is confident in his actions and not sneaking away quietly to do something he does not want the offender to know about. The offender is going to be able to see the officer writing the summons in his rear view mirror anyway, so tell the offender what is planned while standing in a ready position. That way, the officer will be able to respond to whatever reaction the offender may have.

It is not against the law for the violator to exit his vehicle. The officer cannot order him to remain in his vehicle, but the direction can sound like an order. It is merely a directive, what the officer wants the operator to do. The operator is free to exit his vehicle as long as he does not threaten or impede the officer or present a danger to himself or others.

During the entire duration of the stop, the officer's weapon hand should be positioned in the area of his weapon and his body should always be bladed toward the violator.

The officer returns to his vehicle in the same path he approached. He should remain vigilant in watching the occupants. He must be extra careful crossing between the vehicles because now the operator will not be surprised by this movement.

Upon re-entering the unit the officer should advise dispatch of his status ("Unit 123 to headquarters—Ok and issuing"). The officer should make any adjustments to vehicle positioning he deems necessary. The unit's driver's window should be down and AM/FM radio should be off. The officer is now charged with the task of completing the summons while remaining attentive to any potentially dangerous stimuli.

The greatest threat to the officer is still the vehicle occupants. The officer should be very familiar with the motor vehicle summons and pre-decide where he will stop writing and glance up to check on the occupants. Most summonses can be divided into four parts—*operator information, vehicle information, violation information* and *court information.* These natural breaks in the summons can be used as points where the officer looks up to check on the status of the occupants.

The officer should write the summons at the "3PM" position on the steering wheel. This is a comfortable position to write in and allows visual surveillance of the suspect vehicle. The officer can maintain a better surveillance on the offending vehicle by getting vehicle information by looking at the offending vehicle rather than looking down at the registration. The vehicle make, model, body type, color and registration can all be obtained by merely looking through the windshield. Use of this technique minimizes the time the officer is looking down and creates more time of observing the vehicle and its occupants.

The officer should also check the surrounding area, including his rear view mirror to ensure no dangers are present or emerging. There should never be a situation where anyone approaches the unit without the officer's foreknowledge or the offending vehicle departs the scene without the officer's knowledge. (If an officer is approaching another officer's unit as backup, he should knock on the rear quarter panel as he approaches so the other officer is not startled by his appearance.)

If an occupant exits the offending vehicle and begins to approach, the officer has two options. The officer can exit his vehicle, assume a ready stance behind the concealment of his opened front door and interact with the subject. Better yet, the officer should back up approximately two car lengths, advise dispatch, and then exit the vehicle. The distance will allow the officer more time to observe the approaching occupant's attitude and demeanor and to better assess the entire situation. The occupant should be ordered back into the offending vehicle where the officer can conduct the interaction from a position of tactical advantage. The officer must be aware not only of the approaching occupant but all the other occupants and circumstances present. This is often best achieved from a distance.

If, for some reason, the officer does allow the occupant to approach the unit, the occupant should be directed to speak to the officer from the passenger side window (occupant away from the officer, occupant away from traffic). The passenger door should be locked and the window lowered about 1/3.

The summons should be completed in ballpoint pen and be neat and legible. A summons is a court document and should be completed with care. The officer should print everything except his name. When signing the summons, the officer should include his rank, his first initial, last name and badge number (Off. J. Smith #123). An officer does not want to include his first name; this may lend a sense of informality to future interactions.

When a defendant approaches an officer in court he should refer to the officer by rank, not by first name.

The officer should complete all information required including court information and penalty schedule. A return date should be chosen consistent with departmental and court policies but ten to fourteen days for answering a motor vehicle summons is a good rule of thumb.

Service of the Summons

Once the summons has been completed the officer should plan what tactics he will use for *service of the summons*. Before exiting the vehicle the officer should take the same steps he initially took when approaching the vehicle (Exit the Patrol Vehicle). The officer should scan the area for any potential dangers. The officer should approach the vehicle with the same level of caution he did on the initial approach. Officers often make the mistake of assuming that once the ticket is written the stop is over. This can be a fatal mistake. The occupants of the vehicle have had approximately five minutes alone to discuss their situation and formulate a plan. The officer must proceed with caution.

The officer should approach the vehicle on the passenger side. Again, distance is an officer's friend. A hostile reaction from the operator is better handled from the passenger side. Whether the reaction is anger or aggression the distance provided by the passenger side approach will serve the officer well. Again, the officer must use extra care in crossing between the vehicles because the element of surprise no longer exists.

The occupants are contacted in the same manner and with the same level of caution as the initial approach. The officer should stay back near the doorjamb as he explains the enforcement action. This puts the officer at a position of tactical advantage and causes the operator to have to turn his neck uncomfortably to face the officer. Unless the officer detects a suspicious circumstance, there is no reason to move forward to the windshield area during this phase of the stop. It is unlikely the offender has moved contraband into plain view while waiting for the officer to write a summons.

Summons is served from the passenger side, with the offender having to reach out toward the tactically positioned officer

Paperwork and enforcement action should be presented with the support hand. At no time should the officer's weapon hand be encumbered with paperwork. The operator should have to reach for the paperwork as opposed to the officer reaching into the vehicle. If the operator refuses the paperwork, it can be dropped on the passenger seat. If the passenger window is rolled up and the offender refuses to roll it down and receive the summons, the officer must make a reasonable effort to serve the summons. This would most commonly include placing the summons and credentials under the windshield wiper on the passenger side like a parking ticket. As a last resort, the summons can be mailed to the offender.

When the offender receives the summons, the officer should explain the summons quickly and professionally. He should basically have a pre-arranged speech that explains the operator's options. Usually the operator can either pay the ticket or plead not guilty. Both options should be clearly explained. Make sure the operator knows he has the right to plead not guilty and go to court. This demonstrates to the offender that the officer is confident in his enforcement actions and the threat of a court appearance does not bother him.

The offender should then be provided with a brief period to ask any questions. The officer must control this portion of the stop to ensure it does not digress into an argument or street trial. Any legitimate concerns should be addressed but the information the operator needs is contained within the summons and has been explained.

Clear the Scene

The officer should direct the offender to wear his seatbelt and *clear the scene*. The wearing of the seatbelt may be a lawful order (depending on State law); the departing of the scene is another direction phrased as an order. If the offender is legally parked, he does not have to leave the scene. Either way, the officer is responsible for the well-being of the operator and should allow reasonable time for the operator to re-enter traffic. An officer may have to take special care in assisting motorists back into the flow of traffic; this may include an escort into the right lane of a highway with emergency lights activated or actually stopping traffic to allow a frightened violator back into the lane of travel.

The threat is still present until the offender returns to traffic and departs the scene.

The officer will have to make notes about the stop on his copy of the summons, log the stop on his patrol chart and call back into service. This should generally constitute a reasonable amount of time for the offender to re-enter traffic.

The court's copy of the summons should be dropped off prior to the conclusion of the tour of duty or early the next day.

CHAPTER 2

Variations of the Basic Unknown-Risk Stop

Circumstances or personal preference may preclude the use of the passenger side approach. Variations of the passenger side approach are presented for officer's consideration. The officer should practice all methods of vehicle approach to the point where he is familiar with each. He can then decide which method best serves his needs and also has working knowledge of other methods of approach should a situation necessitate their use.

Basic Unknown-Risk Stop from the Driver's side

All procedures previously listed are the same. The officer should take extra care with positioning of the vehicle to ensure the presence of the "safety zone" created by aligning his right headlight with the center of the offending vehicle. The officer must also take extra care as he walks around the front of his car because his vehicle position, while creating the "safety zone," forces the officer to walk closer to the right lane of traffic.

As the officer approaches the offending vehicle, he is still concentrating on the occupant's hands. The trunk check and back seat glance are the same. The officer should use the offending vehicle's left exterior mirror to assist in viewing the operator. If the officer cannot see the operator's hand, a verbal direction (in the form of a polite request) should be issued to show the hands (e.g. "May I see your hands, please?"). Failure to comply heightens the threat level.

Initial contact should be from the doorjamb area, behind the operator's left shoulder. It should be extremely uncomfortable for the operator to turn to look at the officer and nearly impossible for the operator to touch the officer.

Most drivers stow paperwork in the glove box or center console so the officer should be ready to move to a better position of observation as the driver moves for required paperwork.

Once the officer is certain the offender's hands are clear, the offender should be directed to obtain pertinent paperwork. As the offender opens his glove box to obtain the paperwork, the officer moves into a position where he can see the offender's hands and the contents of the glove box.

Upon receiving the paperwork with the support hand, quickly reviewing it and storing it in a pocket, the officer may want to move to an area just in front of the left exterior mirror to facilitate a plain view search of the vehicle's front seat area. The officer must be aware that moving to the front of the vehicle allows more of a view of the vehicle interior but also exposes more of the officer's body mass as a potential target; the officer is also more vulnerable to the vehicle being swung to the left and striking the officer or pushing him into traffic.

As the offender explains why he committed the violation, the officer moves up to facilitate his plain view search of the vehicle interior.

Officers pre-planning for a possible assault must be aware of the fact that windshield glass is not the same as the glass on the rest of the vehicle. Side and rear window glass are made of tempered glass which is approximately ten times stronger than regular glass. This allows the windows to deflect hailstones and other impacts that would break regular glass. When a bullet is fired into tempered glass, the glass shatters completely and the bullet stays on target.

Windshield glass is made of laminated glass. It is a process where a piece of polyvinyl butyral is placed between two pieces of glass and heated. This process of making windshield glass as well as the angle of the windshield forces a downward trajectory of bullets fired into a vehicle. Bullets fired into a vehicle may drop as much as six inches as they enter the occupant area of the vehicle. Officers must be aware of this and take it into consideration before a firefight commences (Rayburn, 2002). For an excellent review of this topic an officer should consult *Advanced Vehicle Stop Tactics* by Michael T. Rayburn.

The officer should **secure pertinent paperwork, issue the summons** and **serve the summons** as previously outlined.

If the officer senses a negative reaction upon the service of the summons, he may want to create space by approaching on the passenger side.

The Call Out

In *Pennsylvania v. Mimms* (1977) the United States Supreme Court noted "the inordinate risk confronting an officer as he approaches a person seated in an automobile." It is for this reason the Court allows officers to remove any lawfully stopped operator from his vehicle. The Court allows the officer to conduct the stop from a safe location close by. All the officer needs is a general concern for his safety, and that concern level is less then the legal threshold of reasonable suspicion. There does not have to be the suspicion that any criminal activity is being undertaken. Unidentified occupants that have been fully concealed from the officer, in an area (vehicle interior) with which they are familiar is generally a matter of concern. The vehicle interior can be altered or stocked to contain any number of threats. These factors are enough to warrant the removal of an operator for the purpose of conducting a motor vehicle stop. Still, each officer must be sure to check his State's interpretation of this Supreme Court decision for applicability in his jurisdiction.

The call out can be a highly effective lawful enforcement tool. It is firmly grounded on Supreme Court decisions. It is not recommended for every stop because of the offender's exposure to passing traffic but in special cases it is very useful.

As always the officer's paramount concern is the protection of human life, so if the call out is going to be employed the officer must take extra care to ensure the offender can exit his vehicle safely and the area where the contact is conducted is safe.

The call out works well with any vehicle that limits the officer's view of the interior (SUV's, vans, box trucks), vehicles with tinted windows or vehicles with many occupants. It allows the officer to concentrate his attention on one occupant at a time. The mentality behind the call out can also be easily adapted to other law enforcement situations such as the operator exiting the vehicle without being asked or an officer approaching an apparent disabled vehicle with occupants already out of the vehicle. The call out is very rarely used and will come as a surprise to the operator. It will also negate any nasty surprise the occupants may have had for the officer in the vehicle. The call out obviously limits the officer's plain view search of the vehicle interior. At some point, when the officer feels safe, he should approach the vehicle for his plain view/plain scent search.

The techniques already outlined are used up to the point of *approach of the vehicle.* With the unit in a left off set position and both vehicles at a complete stop, the officer should engage the unit's PA system. If the PA is not working, strong verbal commands can be substituted.

The officer should open the driver's side door, exit the unit and stand in the area between the open door and the body of the car. This position exposes the officer to the danger of traffic so he may want to re-position the vehicle more toward the right side of the roadway (the unit should also be far enough back from the offending vehicle that the officer has time to enter the unit and back up if rushed by the occupants). The officer should be standing behind the unit's driver side door, in a bladed position

with his strong hand on his weapon and the PA microphone in his support hand.

The officer should use brief, simple commands. Have the operator lower the driver's side window. Direct the operator to obtain pertinent paperwork and hold it in his left hand outside of the vehicle. When this has been completed, direct the operator to exit the vehicle and slowly walk to the rear of his vehicle and lean/sit on the center of his trunk.

As the operator is walking back the officer is conducting an intensive plain view search. As the operator is

walking back the officer may want to direct him to carry the paperwork in his right hand, as this will encumber the hand the vast majority of citizens primarily use to shoot with.

The officer wants the operator off the left side of the roadway and to the center rear of the offending vehicle as quickly as possible (in deference to traffic). With the operator at the center rear of his vehicle the officer can give instructions to other vehicle occupants. "Stay still" would be a minimum order, although circumstances may dictate the officer direct the occupants to place their hands in a more tactically advantageous position (out the window, behind their heads, on the roof, etc.).

The officer can put the microphone down (not wrapped around the steering wheel) and conduct the stop in normal voice tones. The officer may approach the operator or have the operator get in a position of further tactical disadvantage (on his knees, hands on the hood of the unit, etc). The officer wants to keep the offender near the offending vehicle; if the offender gets too close to the unit the officer will no longer be able to keep the offending vehicle and its occupants in his peripheral vision. The officer should never turn his back on the suspect vehicle.

Prior to approaching the offender, the officer may want the offender to move to the right rear quarter panel of the offending vehicle. This will allow the officer to step out from behind his cover/concealment and approach the offender with a physical barrier still present (the right angle created by the trunk of the offender's vehicle). To maintain this physical barrier the stop may be conducted across the trunk of the offending vehicle.

The right angle created by the vehicle's trunk provides a physical barricade between the officer and the offending operator.

With vans, SUVs, work trucks, etc., the officer may want to have the offender open the rear doors prior to leaving cover/concealment.

If the officer decides to interview vehicle occupants he must approach the vehicle with the utmost of caution. He should advise the operator and dispatch of his intentions. Credentials should be stowed as the officer walks up the right side of the vehicle approximately 2 arm lengths behind the operator. The officer should direct the operator to walk to the front center of the offending vehicle, approximately one body width away from the vehicle; this position will not obstruct the officer's use of the right exterior mirror to observe the occupants. As he walks by, the operator should be directed to tell the right rear passenger to "Open the door." With a sedan type vehicle the operator should be directed to sit on the hood of the car facing away from the vehicle, feet up on the bumper, hands clasped together with the chin resting in the hands. From this position the officer can watch the operator and any movements can be detected by sight or touch (when the vehicle moves). With vans or SUVs the operator should be placed near the right headlight (within the officer's view) with his hands resting on the vehicle.

The driver is seated on the hood with his elbows on his knees and his chin in his hand. He is in a relatively comfortable position but a position of tactical disadvantage. The officer has a clear view of all the occupants' hands though they can not see him.

The officer should now be in a position near the right rear tire. He should be able to peer into the vehicle interior without exposing his body mass to an attack from the right rear passenger. As he completes this phase of his investigation and slowly moves forward, he should direct the front passenger to open the front passenger door. The officer should continue the stop from the right doorjamb area but approximately 3 feet back from the vehicle. From this position he can hear the occupants and he can watch the operator and occupants.

The officer can see and hear all the vehicle occupants while still observing the operator on the hood.

The officer can interview the operator out of earshot of the occupants but with the occupants still within his view. The officer should position himself about 2 feet left of the operator on the hood. From this position a physical attack from the operator is very difficult, the officer can speak and hear the operator and still maintain a good surveillance on the vehicle occupants.

If the operator is to be arrested, the officer should wait for backup. If waiting for backup is not practicable the officer should verbally order the operator into a position of tactical disadvantage (on the knees, cross your ankles, sit back on your ankles, hands behind your back). The officer can maintain a visual surveillance on the vehicle occupants as he handcuffs and then searches his arrestee.

When the interview with the occupants is complete, the operator should be directed back into the vehicle or directed to remain near the hood of his car as enforcement action is taken.

The other mechanics of the stop would remain the same. The summons can be served by approaching the vehicle or having the operator exit his vehicle.

Removal of Passengers

The U.S. Supreme Court considered the removal of passengers in *Maryland v. Wilson* (1997). The Court appreciated the presence of danger presented by passengers. Individual State laws may be more restrictive but per the

United States Supreme Court, passengers can be removed during the course of a motor vehicle stop.

If a passenger makes an overtly suspicious movement he would be removed first. But in the majority of cases, the driver will be removed first. The driver should be brought to the left-front of the offending vehicle and seated on the hood with his hands on his knees. The passengers should be directed to sit with their elbows on their knees with their chins resting in their hands. This is a somewhat relaxed tactical position to leave the passengers in, as opposed to hands interlocked on the head or palms pushed to the ceiling. The passenger is comfortable and does not feel like a criminal but the officer still can see the passenger's hands; the passengers would have to make an obvious movement to retrieve any item from the vehicle interior or their person.

With the driver seated above the left headlight the officer can interview the driver and maintain strong visual surveillance on the vehicle interior. The officer should be far enough back from the seated operator (about 3 feet) to discourage a sudden physical attack.

Once the interview of the driver is concluded, the officer should direct the operator to remain seated with his elbows on his knees, hands clasped together, with his chin resting in his hands. The officer can move around to the passenger side of the vehicle. If there is a rear seat passenger the officer takes up a position behind the rear passenger, about parallel to the right rear tire. From this position the officer can interview the rear passenger while maintaining a visual on the driver and front passenger. Once the interview is complete the officer would step to the right and forward so he can interview the front passenger and maintain a view of the rear passenger and the driver.

After these interviews the officer will make a determination if there is probable cause a crime has been committed. If the officer determines there is probable cause, he should update dispatch and request backup. The officer should wait for backup to arrive before proceeding. If, for some reason, the officer cannot wait for backup he must move the vehicle occupants to a more secure position. If the rear of the unit has a cage, that is where the officer should begin to move the most suspicious (dangerous) of the occupants. The officer should open the unit's driver side door and stand next to the unit, behind the door. The officer should use simple verbal commands to move one occupant at a time to the right front of the unit. The occupant should be directed to place his hands on the right side of the hood of the unit (just above the front tire, feet back). This is the traditional position and it works well. Some seasoned offenders have trained to attack officers from this position. Also, the officer has to be forceful in ensuring the offender's feet are far enough back from the unit, otherwise the offender can gain momentum in attacking the officer by pushing back off the unit. A better position is to have the offender (hands in the small of his back) put his feet back far enough from the unit, that he can rest his head on the trunk. Another position of tactical advantage for the officer is have the offender kneel on the ground, hands on his head, then sit back on his ankles.

A motivated or highly trained offender can counter the traditional search position.

An attack is much more difficult to launch from this position.

The officer approaches the suspect while looking at the offending vehicle. The suspect is handcuffed, then searched. It is always, "Cuff, then Search." The suspect is placed in the rear of the unit.

The rear of the unit should hold two handcuffed occupants comfortably. The rear doors should be locked, securing the occupants, as the officers choose their next course of action.

The arrestee is directed to enter the rear of the unit as the officer maintains visual surveillance on the vehicle occupants.

Basic Unknown-Risk Stop Elevates to a High-Risk Stop

During the motor vehicle stop, the officer is constantly re-assessing the threat level. Factors may change or develop, which escalate an unknown-risk stop into a high-risk stop. These factors include:

1) presence of a weapon
2) information from dispatch connecting the vehicle or occupants with felonious behavior
3) physically aggressive occupants
4) any other factor the officer can articulate that heightens the threat level

If at least one of these factors is present, the officer must adjust his thinking pattern and get into the high-risk stop mode. In order to safely conduct a high-risk stop, the officer is going to need *distance* and *assistance*.

The officer should immediately return to the unit and back up about 25 feet (from 10 feet back, the unit is now 35 feet back). The officer should direct dispatch to send backup and advise of the situation.

Upon completion of these tasks, the officer should follow the procedures outlined in the next chapter, beginning with positioning of the unit. At this time, the officer is the primary unit. Traffic and road conditions permitting, the officer should position his unit at a 35-degree angle to the left curb, with the doorjamb aligned with the center of the suspect vehicle.

• Direct the occupants to remain in the vehicle.

• Step out of the unit and assume a kneeling, strong hand barricaded position behind the front tire.

• Unless the occupants force action, wait for backup.

CHAPTER 3

High-risk stops

 high-risk stop is any stop where factors known to the officer lead to the reasonable belief that:

1) he is dealing with persons prone to assault
2) the vehicle or occupants are engaging in or have been involved in a felony
3) any other facts that can be articulated by the officer which heighten the threat level

The officer should prepare for a high-risk stop every day by:

1) mentally noting appropriate stop locations
2) thinking of what will be said in what order
3) pre-planning where he wants officers positioned during each phase of the stop

Upon recognizing he is dealing with a high-risk stop situation, the officer must advise dispatch and request all other radio communications, not related to the stop, cease or be taken to another channel. The officer should communicate as much pertinent information as possible. He must request backup officers and find out from where the officers are responding. This will give him a gauge of their estimated time of arrival and allow the officer to begin to visualize safe locations where the stop could be conducted.

The presence of backup is the most important factor in a high-risk stop. The second most important factor is the location. The officer must be aware that there will be several units, possibly from different jurisdictions, responding. Weapons will be present and will be drawn. The officer should consider that shots may be fired so he must think of the background. The officer must select a location as far from civilian population as possible that will accommodate a large number of police units responding from different locations. The selected location should be known to other officers and accessible. Ideal locations would include an industrial park at night, a mall in off hours or a large parking lot.

Once the location has been mentally selected the officer should advise the responding officers. He should advise of the direction of travel and his planned entry point. This will allow responding officers to plan their approach to ensure they are properly situated.

The officer should not initiate the stop until two other units are present. Once the units are present and advised of the plan (who will go right, who will go left) and dispatch is notified, all units should activate their overhead lights and sirens. Hopefully, the offending vehicle will stop when the lights are activated in the location pre-selected.

Whether the suspect vehicle stops at the pre-selected location or not, once it comes to rest the next steps are the same. Space permitting, the units want to park in a staggered line, at an angle with the suspect vehicle, approximately 30-40 feet back.

Traditionally, the units have stopped directly behind the suspect's vehicle; officers have positioned themselves in the area between the unit's open driver's side door and the body of the unit. This position provides the officer with concealment but not much cover. The door of a police unit will not stop many high-powered rounds. The engine block will stop rounds but only a small portion of the officer's body is behind the engine block. If a suspect exits his vehicle shooting, the officer loses the cover from his unit. Most of the patrol unit's body is made of fiberglass or thin steel that offers little protection for the officer. Also, the officer's feet are not protected from skipping rounds and very limited as to where he can move laterally. The officer is in the uncomfortable *left side barricaded* shooting position. Other assisting officers are limited as to where they can position themselves to assist.

The first unit (the left assist unit) should pull to the left of the suspect vehicle at a 35 degree angle with the left curb; the unit's front tire and engine block should be on a 45-degree angle from the suspect vehicle's driver's door. For the driver to shoot at the left unit, he should have to turn almost all the way around. The front tires should be cut to the right in case the unit has to be moved quickly. This will provide the officer a larger area behind his unit to observe the suspect vehicle and still allow him to pull out quickly if need be.

The second unit (middle unit) should pull in at an angle on the passenger side of the left assist unit. The second unit should be at a 35-degree angle to the left curb. The left front of the unit should be at least three feet from the left vehicle's rear passenger bumper (to provide a walkway between the units). The second unit's passenger doorjamb should be aligned with the center of the suspect vehicle.

The third unit should pull in at an angle next to the center unit (to the right or to the left). The third unit should be at a 35-degree angle with the left curb. The front of the unit should be at least three feet from the center unit's rear bumper. The unit's engine block should be aligned with the suspect vehicle's passenger door. For the passenger to shoot at the right unit, he would have to turn almost all the way around. In a case where the suspect vehicle stops along the right curb, the right assist vehicle will have to pull parallel to the right curb; if the right assist slants to the center, the officer will not have a clear view of suspect's right passenger door.

The units should not be directly behind each other but rather slanted and staggered, similar to parking spaces at the mall. The units may overlap, but that is not a bad thing.

The officers will exit their vehicles quickly and assume a strong hand, kneeling, barricade position behind the front tires of their units. Based on the distance, a long weapon is better then a hand gun if the choice exists.

By crouching behind a unit's front tire, the officer can use the engine block as cover and concealment. The two tires would provide some cover from rounds fired at the ground, certainly more cover than the traditional position. The officers would be spread further apart, giving them a better angle of visibility of the suspect vehicle. Officers can move laterally along the body of the units with cover being provided by the passenger side and driver side. Responding officers would have a better choice of positioning along the length of the left assist and primary units. Officers will also have better access to the unit's trunk in case other weapons are stored there.

The vehicle in the center should be the primary unit— the unit conducting the stop. This may not be the officer who initially observed the suspect vehicle but rather the unit occupied by the officer whose training and experience has best prepared him for a high-risk stop situation.

The units should de-activate the siren but leave the overhead lights on. Any supplemental lights such as spotlights and alley lights should be shone on the suspect vehicle.

A high-risk stop is a very stressful situation. The officer must train himself to relax. Time is on the side of the officer. More officers, weapons and resources are coming.

The primary unit will be giving strong verbal commands to the suspects and to other officers via the unit's PA system. Prior to getting into this situation the officer should make sure there is enough wire attached to the PA microphone to reach the front tire area. Otherwise, the officer may have to use a megaphone, a strong voice or give up some cover to be closer to the radio.

The vehicle operator, the vehicle occupants and the vehicle itself all present separate threats to the officer. The instructions should be designed to incrementally lower the threat of each risk. The goal is to have all occupants laying facing down in the area between the units and the suspect vehicle, with their hands cuffed behind their backs and ankles crossed.

The primary officer should use clear, simple, brief commands. No order should be given until the previous order has been complied with completely. The primary officer should start each command with the person the order is directed toward. Only one person should be moving at a time and all persons present (officers and suspects) should know who that person is. Between each order there should be a 2-3 second delay to ensure compliance and allow updates from the assisting officers:

1) "Driver, turn off the car"

2) "Driver, throw the keys out the window"

3) "Driver, put both hands outside the window"

4) "Front passenger, put both hands out the window"

5) "Driver, open your door from the outside"

6) "Driver, place your feet on the ground"

7) "Driver, face the hood of your car"

8) "Driver, place your hands above your head"

9) "Driver, leave your door open"

10) "Driver, walk backwards toward the police units"

If the suspect vehicle is a four door, the driver may be stopped and directed to open the left rear door, then continue back. This will allow the officer clearing the vehicle later to have a view of the vehicle interior from a distance. If there is an armed suspect on the back seat he will have to exit the vehicle and shoot around the driver. This procedure can also be used with a van.

At this point, the left assist unit should have his weapon trained on the driver. The right assist officer should have his weapon trained on the front passenger. The primary officer should have his weapon trained on the driver but be visually scanning the front passenger. When the driver gets to the area approximately 25 feet behind his vehicle (10 feet from the officers) the primary officer should order:

11) "Driver, stop"

12) "Driver, turn around slowly"

(Visual weapons check negative)

13) "Driver, face your vehicle"

14) "Driver, get on your knees"

15) "Driver, sit back on your ankles"

16)   "Driver, place both hands on the ground"

17)   "Driver, lower your chest to the pavement"

18)   "Driver, lay flat on your stomach, arms stretched out to the side"

19)   "Driver, cross your ankles"

20)   "Driver, do not move"

21)   "Left assist, cover the driver"

The left assist officer has his weapon trained on the prone driver. The right assist officer has his weapon trained on the front passenger. The front passenger is now more of a risk than the driver so the primary officer has his weapon trained on the front passenger, while still scanning the vehicle and the prone driver. The primary officer may want to move to his unit's rear tire area to obtain a better visual and more direct communication with the passenger.

22)   "Right assist, are you ready?"

23)   "Yes, sir"

24)   "Front passenger, open your door from the outside"

The primary officer would repeat the same orders to the front passenger until the front passenger is prone, next to the driver.

Have the front passenger leave the passenger door open.

If other passengers are present, they are ordered out in the same manner. All occupants should leave the doors open. Even if no other vehicle occupants can be seen, give orders as if there is an occupant present. This bluff may convince the unseen occupant that he has been located and he may give himself up.

With all known occupants out of the vehicle, prone on the ground, the officers face a critical juncture. They must leave cover and concealment to handcuff the suspects but they cannot be 100% sure the vehicle is clear. This is why the occupants were ordered so close to the units.

The suspects should be approached one at a time, by two officers.

With the assisting officer ready to approach the primary officer will order:

25) "Driver and passenger, place your hands on the small of your back"

The officers must be very careful prior to moving out from behind cover because if the suspect has a gun in the small of his back it can be easily accessed now. This threat is weighed against the swiftness the officers can handcuff the suspect and the lack of contact the officer will have to have with the suspect. The primary officer may want to let the suspects lay in that position for a minute to see if they make any movements. When all is determined to be safe, the officers are sent in to handcuff the suspects.

A very brief search of the lower back area may be conducted but the officers are most concerned with getting back to cover. Remember, it is not yet certain the vehicle is unoccupied. Leave the suspects handcuffed on the pavement. They will be moved at a later time.

Now the greatest threat is the vehicle interior and its unknown contents. A field interview should be conducted from cover asking the handcuffed suspects if anyone else is in the car. An answer in the negative is still not enough to assume the vehicle is unoccupied. If the suspects indicate the vehicle is still occupied the primary officer should verbally command the occupant, by name, to exit the vehicle. Hopefully, now that his presence has been confirmed, he will give up. If he does not, the primary officer must assess what resources are available to him. He should request a weapon that is specially designed to fire Oleoresin Capsicum (OC) rounds. Based on information obtained in the field interview, approach the suspect vehicle from the most tactically advantageous side; a unit should be driven very slowly with the OC marksman walking next to the engine block. One step in front of the OC marksman should be a cover officer carrying a rifle. From a distance of approximately 10 feet, 3-5 balls filled with OC should be shot against the interior of the windshield. This application of OC should force the suspect out of the vehicle.

If the suspects indicate the vehicle is unoccupied, an approach is still going to have to be made. Assume the vehicle is occupied and approach with the utmost of caution. Assume approach will be from the left (vehicles are driven on the right side of the roadway and the suspect vehicle should be stopped on the right curb or to the right side of the roadway leaving the left side clear for approach). The primary officer should assess the entire situation and decide from which side the approach will be made. Utilizing a cover unit, place one officer next to the front passenger tire and one officer next to the rear passenger tire. The unit should slowly approach until it is next to the suspect vehicle.

The unit operator may want to drive with the door open to facilitate a quick egress if necessary. If a shoot-out starts, the unit operator will exit the unit, assume a position of cover behind the unit and return fire.

With the unit next to the suspect vehicle but as far to the left as possible, the officers should have a clear view of the vehicle interior because of the open doors. With cover provided by the vehicle, the two officers will have to move into a position where they can visually then physically clear the vehicle of occupants.

Once all previously unseen occupants have been removed and placed in a position of tactical disadvantage, one officer holsters his weapon as two others approach, handcuff and search.

With the interior deemed to be clear the officers should release the trunk and make sure it is empty. The officers should then return to the original position. A complete vehicle search for contraband will be conducted a short time later.

By positioning the approaching unit far to the left, the units in the original stop position can still have weapons trained on the suspect vehicle with the handcuffed suspects in peripheral vision. The approaching unit should form a right angle with the primary officer's vehicle. When the suspect vehicle is deemed clear and the officers are about to leave cover to approach the vehicle, weapons from the primary position should be holstered.

If prevailing circumstances forbid an approach from either side, approach must be made from directly behind the suspect vehicle. Again, one officer should operate a unit, providing cover and concealment to two officers who approach on foot. When the officers clear the unit and approach on foot they still want to expose as little of their bodies as possible to the unknown vehicle interior. A safer approach can be achieved by utilizing a small mirror that attaches to the end of the expandable ASP baton. This mirror is detachable and portable and will allow an officer to see into the vehicle without a full approach.

With the vehicle cleared, attention should be turned back to the prone, handcuffed suspects. Two officers should approach each suspect, weapons holstered (the suspect's hands should be in plain view). The handcuffs should now be double locked. One officer should apply moderate pressure to the upper back area as the other officer conducts a search incident to arrest on the back side of the suspect. When this search is complete, the suspect will be rolled on his back where a similar search will be conducted on his front side. Officers MUST be extremely diligent and systematic in this search. When one officer has completed a search, the officers should reverse roles and another complete search should be conducted by the other officer. Upon completion of the search, the suspects should be placed in the rear of separate units for transport.

A search of the vehicle will be conducted and all evidence should be collected at the scene prior to its removal.

One concern with high-risk stops is the presence of *too many* officers. Everyone wants to help but it is difficult to execute a plan with an ever-changing, ever growing cast of characters. Each of the three original officers (primary, left assist, right assist) should have one backup officer with them. The backup officer should remain nearby, behind cover, close enough to speak to and hear the officer they are assisting. These secondary assist officers on each side must be ready to remain quiet and take orders from the primary officer or the officer they are assisting. The original three officers at the scene may have to exercise some discipline and struggle with other egos to maintain control; some feathers may be ruffled. But it is much easier to smooth some ruffled feathers after a scene is over than work through a high risk situation where seven different officers are doing seven different things. Everyone means well but only one officer can be in control of the scene.

Reality Check

The Officer Down Memorial Page Remembers...

Police Officer Robert J. Stanze II

St. Louis Police Department
Missouri
End of Watch: Tuesday, August 8, 2000

Biographical Info
Age: 29
Tour of Duty: 6 yrs
Badge Number: Not available

Incident Details
Cause of Death: Gunfire
Date of Incident: Tuesday, August 8, 2000
Weapon Used: Handgun
Suspect Info: Sentenced to life

Officer Stanze was shot and killed while arresting a suspect wanted in a shooting of another officer. Officer Stanze and another officer had handcuffed the suspect and placed him in the back of the cruiser. The suspect then drew a handgun he had hidden and opened fire on the officers while they were standing outside. Officer Stanze, who was wearing his bulletproof vest, was struck in the side and the round entered his torso between the two panels. The second officer returned fire, wounding the suspect. In December 2001, the suspect pled guilty and was sentenced to life. Officer Stanze had been with the St. Louis Police Department for six years. He is survived by his wife, who is expectant with twins, and a child.

CHAPTER 4

Approaching Unusual Vehicles

Motorcycles

Motorcycles are quicker and more agile than police cars. This presents problems to officers until the vehicle is at rest. Then the officer holds the tactical advantage.

Motorcycles do present an elevated threat for the following reasons:

1) Many motorcyclists carry their own tools in case they need to make repairs on the road. These tools are stowed on various parts of the motorcycle, including mounted near the front handlebars. This gives the cyclist access to potentially dangerous weapons. Some violent motorcycle gang members exploit the "hands-on repair" culture and carry ball peen hammers. The hammers are supposedly to assist in repairs but there are many more stories of the hammers being used as weapons than there are of the hammers being used to repair anything.

2) The culture of motorcyclists makes vehicle alteration a common thing. Motorcyclists are proud of their rides and spend a great deal of time and money altering the bikes to their personal likings. This knowledge and access to customizing equipment can lead to hidden compartments, sharpened bike parts or even booby trapped areas on the motorcycle.

3) Motorcyclists "dress for the fall, not for the ride." Motorcycle clothing is designed to be durable, protect the rider and allow the rider to carry many items. The pants and especially the jacket have extra pockets that can be used to

carry legal or illegal objects. The extra padding provides the cyclists with protection from falls but would also lessen the impact of physical force and baton strikes from an officer.

4) Common dress includes heavy chains, thick belts, metal belt buckles, heavy boots, thick bracelets, helmets, padded gloves and many rings. These decorative/protective items can become dangerous weapons in the hands of a motivated offender.

5) True "outlaw" motorcycle club riders (1%'ers) are confirmed violent criminals. They seldom ride alone. They discuss interactions with the police and formulate plans to handle different situations. Many are involved in the drug trade or other illegal enterprises. They are violent offenders whom the police must approach with the utmost of caution.

The techniques for stopping a motorcycle are identical to stopping a car. Follow the same procedures outlined in Chapter 1 with a little more care given to location. Soft shoulders, puddles, oil slicks, gravel or sand present hazards to motorcycle riders and should be avoided.

Upon exiting the unit, the officer should use the PA to direct the motorcyclist to turn off the bike. This order may not be heard due to excessive noise from the engine, a helmeted operator and distance. If the order is not heard or ignored, the officer should approach the motorcycle on the right side and use a hand gesture to have the operator turn off the bike.

The stop should be conducted from the right side, body bladed, slightly behind the operator (about even with the rear seat). This will make it difficult for the operator to attack the officer but affords the officer a full view of the operator.

With the motorcycle turned off, the officer should have the operator remove his helmet. This is for identification purposes and enhances communication. Decide where the operator is to store the helmet. A helmet held in the left hand encumbers the hand but a helmet being swung at an officer is a very real threat. The operator should place the helmet on the left handlebar or better yet, the ground on the left side of the bike (if he can reach the ground).

The officer should not allow the operator to put the kick stand down or dismount the motorcycle. Sitting on the bike with the kick stand up will force the motorcycle operator to keep the bike balanced with his feet; this will minimize any aggressive offensive maneuvers by the cycle operator.

The motorcycle operator should keep his hands on the handlebars and the passenger should keep his hands on the operator's shoulders until they receive other instructions from the officer.

The officer should obtain the operator's license while the operator is still seated on and balancing the bike.

Officers should be aware the vehicle registration is often stowed in a storage compartment under the seat. Obtaining this paperwork will necessitate the rider dismounting the motorcycle. Almost all riders dismount on the left side of the bike. In preparation for this the officer should move to a position behind the bike toward the left of the rear tire. This will anticipate the rider's post-dismount

position and place the officer in a tactical position with access to his unit.

The officer should ascertain which way the seat will open. Prior to the operator opening the seat the officer can move to a position that will allow him an unobstructed view of this storage area. Once the paperwork has been retrieved the seat can remain open and the operator should be directed to the right front of the motorcycle, near the front tire. The officer should stand on the left side of the bike, near the windshield. The seat being up will discourage the operator from jumping on the bike and departing. The stop should be conducted across the motorcycle, with the officer using the bike as a physical barrier.

The officer uses the motorcycle to create a physical barrier during the stop.

When issuing the summons, it is optimum for the rider to be on the motorcycle, with the engine off, helmet off, balancing the bike. The rider cannot lawfully be ordered into this position but the direction can be given. This is a somewhat uncomfortable position and the officer should use discretion in deciding where he wants the rider as enforcement action is being taken.

The vast majority of motorcycle enthusiasts are not violent, drug-dealing thugs. Unfortunately the officer does not know until the conclusion of the stop what element of the motorcycle culture he is dealing with. Be alert to these and other dangers. Do not allow yourself to be outnumbered and pre-plan the stop so you maintain the tactical edge.

Tractor Trailers (Semi-Trucks)

Tractor trailer operators have a tactical advantage due to the size of their vehicle and the height at which the occupants sit. The officer can take steps to minimize the driver's advantage but must always respect the size, weight and potential damage a feloniously operated tractor trailer can do.

The majority of tractor trailer drivers are professional, law-abiding citizens. They rely on the safe flow of traffic to make their livelihood and respect the efforts of law enforcement. There are more stories of truckers stopping and helping officers than there are of drivers attacking officers. But still, it only takes one violent encounter to end an officer's life and that is the encounter for which the officer must prepare.

The steps in stopping a tractor trailer are the same as outlined in the basic motor vehicle stop in Chapter 1, up to the time of selecting a location. The officer must select a location where the shoulder is wide enough that the truck will be out of the flow of traffic. Avoid soft shoulders where the weight of the truck may cause the vehicle to slide or get stuck. Avoid steep inclines or declines.

The officer must pay extra care in *getting the operator's attention*. After activating emergency lights and siren the officer may have to pull a half-car width to the left so the operator can see the officer in the left rear view mirror. When the operator recognizes he is being stopped, he should respond by slowing down and putting on his right turn indicator; he may also activate his hazard lights. At this point the officer should move a half-car width to the right of the tractor trailer to "escort" him to the right shoulder. It is the blind spot on the right side of the truck that causes the driver the most consternation; the officer should take steps to mitigate this concern and make pulling to the right shoulder as safe as possible. The officer should be somewhat further back with a tractor trailer to keep traffic back as the truck slows to a stop.

The officer will know when the tractor trailer comes to complete rest because the air brakes make a distinctive sound as they are set. With the tractor trailer at full rest the officer has two options:

First, the officer can conduct the stop similar to the "call out" stop. The officer would stand at the left rear of the trailer and motion for the driver to walk back to that location. The officer would be able to observe the driver climbing down from the cab and walking toward him. If anything is amiss, the officer has time to retreat to cover or recover to the unit and create more distance. An alert officer would watch under the passenger side trailer for any passengers who may have decided to come to the rear of the truck.

Another option would have the officer pull out from behind the truck and position his unit approximately 40-50 feet in front of the tractor. The nose of the unit should be at a 35-degree angle to the curb (approximately); this position will create a physical barrier between the officer and the driver but also allow the officer to pull away in an emergency situation. The officer should make sure the rear of the unit is not protruding into the lane of travel.

The positioning of the unit in front of the tractor trailer may seem to be exposing the officer to a greater risk. This approach is the direct opposite of the approach utilized for every other vehicle. But when the risks are considered, the front position may be the safest position for the officer. Approaching from the front, the officer's greatest risk is the driver opening fire without warning. This threat also exists with an approach from the rear. Officers should not be so naïve to think a passenger side approach will surprise a truck driver. Drivers talk to each other and (very innocently) mention police techniques. The officer's passenger approach will not be the driver's first experience with it. Drivers are also experts at using their exterior rear view mirrors to assess traffic on both sides. An officer approaching from the rear on either side will be observed by the trucker.

Reality Check

The Officer Down Memorial Page Remembers...

Master Trooper David Anthony Deuter

Indiana State Police
Indiana
End of Watch: Thursday, July 16, 1998

Biographical Info
Age: 49
Tour of Duty: 26 yrs
Badge Number: Not available

Incident Details
Cause of Death: Struck by vehicle
Date of Incident: Thursday, July 16, 1998
Weapon Used: Automobile; Commercial
Suspect Info: Charged with reckless homicide

Trooper Deuter was killed after being struck by a tractor trailer while making a traffic stop on the Indiana Toll Road in Howe, Indiana. Trooper Deuter was standing next to the driver's side door of the vehicle when he was struck. The suspect was charged with reckless homicide in connection with Trooper Deuter's death. Trooper Deuter had been with the Indiana State Police for 26 years and is survived by his wife and four children.

Advantages of positioning the unit in front of the tractor trailer include:

1) Presence of other occupants. The officer is in a better position to assess the presence of other occupants in cab

2) Less time for the driver to prepare. If the driver was planning an attack, he will have less time to do so because the officer can almost immediately begin visual surveillance.

3) Better view of the cab interior. An officer approaching from the rear is likely to stop in front of the cab, near one of the headlights. He is now looking up into the cab at a very sharp angle. The front positioning of the unit allows the officer a better view into the cab from a safer distance.

4) Contact with the driver. The driver is forced to alight from the cab and approach the officer instead of the officer climbing up the side of the rig to contact the driver.

5) Limited risk from passing traffic. The unit and the officer are protected from passing traffic by the tractor trailer.

It is unlikely the tractor trailer operator will be able to hear the officer, even with the use of the PA. The officer should exit and stand near the unit's left front tire and motion for the driver to come down. As a professional driver, the tractor trailer operator should know what is expected of him and will bring the proper paperwork; failure to do so indicates a new driver or elevates the level of risk.

As the driver is walking toward the unit, the officer should be conducting an intensive visual search of the driver; the officer should also be looking into the cab of the trailer for indications of the presence of another occupant. From here, the stop is conducted the same as a regular call out stop. The officer can remain on the left side of his vehicle, close to an open door and the radio; the driver can stand near the center of the unit's hood. This will allow for clear verbal communication while maintaining a physical barrier and reducing the concern of passing traffic.

If the driver states he has to return to the cab to retrieve anything the officer should escort the driver to the passenger side of the cab. The officer should be 5-6 feet behind the driver as they are walking. Prior to allowing the operator to enter the cab, the driver should be directed to sit on the curb. The officer can then climb up on the right side of the cab and conduct a plain view search. The driver should be seated far enough away from the officer that sudden attack is difficult. Once the cab has been visually cleared the driver can be directed to enter the cab from the driver's side while the officer continues to look into the passenger side window. The driver will be out of the officer's view as he walks from his seated position to the driver's side door. The officer should direct the driver to "show his hands" as soon as he comes into view on the driver's side.

The best position for the officer to prepare any written enforcement action would be with the officer standing near the left front quarter panel of the unit, facing the driver who would be seated in the cab. Any position different than this is trading-off safety for comfort.

The driver should come down out of the cab to receive any written enforcement paperwork. Upon service of the paperwork, the officer should straighten the unit and pull further up the shoulder to allow the tractor trailer to build up speed and re-enter the flow of traffic.

CHAPTER 5

Two-Officer Stops

The presence of a partner is only an advantage if the officers know what is expected of them and know what to expect from each other. The officers should discuss and plan vehicle approach tactics in their down time so when a stop is being conducted there are no nasty surprises.

The main goal of the two-officer stop is to have as many eyes on the occupants as possible but never be in a crossfire. The second goal is to disorient the occupants, especially on the initial approach. The plan is to have the primary officer conduct the stop from the passenger side (just like the basic, unknown-risk stop) with the assisting officer watching the occupants from the front center of the suspect vehicle. This allows both officers a clear view of the occupants, keeps both officers out of traffic and keeps both officers close to cover if needed. Also, if there is any shooting the officers would not be firing anywhere near each other.

This positioning is safer than the traditional "primary officer at the driver's window, assisting officer at the right rear." First off, the dangers an officer is exposed to on the driver's side of a vehicle have already been enumerated. Second, the assisting officer never really gets a good view of the occupants; he is obstructed by the design of the vehicle. If he does move up to look into the vehicle, he no longer forms an "L" with the primary officer and there is a better chance of a crossfire. Even from the original position, if the secondary officer has to shoot into the vehicle he does not have a clear view and he is shooting toward the primary officer. Third, if there is a physical confrontation between the driver and the primary officer or occupants and the secondary officer, the other officer has to run all the way around the suspect vehicle to assist his partner. From the front, the assisting officer is inaccessible to the vehicle occupants and has a clear view of any aggressive actions before the attack is launched. If there is an assault the assisting officer has a short, unobstructed run to assist his partner. The idea of backup is to create a 2 on 1 situation with the advantage to the officers. By standing on opposite sides of the suspect vehicle this advantage is lost. Fourth, both officers are closer to each other (for communication purposes) and are closer to cover.

How the officers get to this position is as important as the final position. Prior to the unit coming to rest, the officers should determine who will be the primary officer and who will be the assisting officer. All aspects of the stop are the same as the basic unknown-risk stop. Upon exiting the unit, the assisting officer should take the lead and approach on the driver's side. As they approach the trunk the primary officer should be only slightly behind the assisting officer on the passenger side.

The secondary officer conducts a brief plain view search of the rear passenger area; by moving forward he silently indicates to the primary officer the area is clear. The secondary officer should knock on the left rear of the offending vehicle to get the occupant's attention. At this time the assisting officer is at the driver's door and the primary officer is near the right rear tire.

As the occupants turn toward the left side of the vehicle to engage the secondary officer, the primary officer moves up to the passenger side doorjamb; from here he conducts a plain view search of the vehicle interior.The secondary officer conducts his own plain view search, concentrating mostly on the driver's hands as he passes the vehicle. As the secondary officer passes, he directs the offender to turn off the engine. He then assumes a position in the front center. All attention is on the secondary officer as he looks into the vehicle interior. When the primary officer is comfortable, he knocks on the front passenger door and conducts the stop on the confused occupants.

The secondary officer may "cheat" a little toward the right side of the front of the offending vehicle, just to be a little closer to his partner and a little closer to cover.

If a summons is to be issued, the secondary officer can remain where he is as the primary officer conducts business safely in the unit. The primary officer must look up periodically to check on the status of his partner.

The primary officer may re-approach the vehicle, secure in the knowledge it is safe because the assisting officer has maintained surveillance on the occupants.

Partners should also work on codes that can surreptitiously make each other aware of a risk without tipping off the suspects. A very easy code is using a partner's full first name when trouble has been detected. This verbal cue will make the partner aware the threat level has been heightened, while not alerting the occupants. For something serious or lethal, like the presence of a weapon, there should be no code; the partner should yell, "Gun" and draw his weapon. That will serve as verbal cue enough.

If one officer is searching a car and the other officer is watching a suspect, the officer who finds evidence wants to get into a good tactical position before announcing his find. The officer should not be bent under the front seat yelling, "I found drugs," as his partner is alone with the suspect. The officer should quietly secure the evidence, then approach the suspect (the suspect should be facing away from the area being searched). The primary officer gives his verbal cue then says something like, "Oh well, Officer/Partner Matthew...nothing in there...you were right, Mr. Suspect...no contraband...do you mind if I do one last pat search?" The relieved suspect willingly complies with the "bumbling" officer, knowing the contraband was under the seat and not on his person. Once the suspect turns his back and puts his hands on the hood, the two officers immediately work as a team to secure the suspect. The officers must use their familiarity with each other to convey information and stay a step ahead of the suspect.

CHAPTER 6

General Safety Guidelines

To promote professionalism and safety, officers should adhere to the following guidelines:

1) *Conduct all stops as if all actions are being videotaped and audio taped.* This is the trend in the profession and if your departmental vehicles are not equipped with video systems, they soon will be. The video is the professional officer's best defense against allegations of racial profiling, illegal behavior and attitude/demeanor complaints.

2) *Be prepared for unusual situations by pre-planning.* While on routine patrol, the officer should visualize worst case scenarios and think of appropriate responses. While waiting at a red light, imagine, "What would I do if an armed gunman ran out of that convenience store right now?" or "What would I do if this guy walking down the street snatched that lady's purse?" or "If this car in front of me was wanted, where would I stop it?" By thinking of different scenarios and having time to formulate responses, an officer will be better prepared when an unusual incident does occur.

    This thinking should be extended to every police situation. As an officer views a video of a police situation, do not just view it passively. View it actively, thinking, "What would I have done?" "What has this officer done well?" "What could be done better?" Most videos involve rare occurrences but by thinking through the situation in low stress conditions or in a class room situation, the officer will be better prepared for decision-making in a high stress or combat situation. Discuss the actions of the officers with other officers in your department. Seek out SWAT members or senior officers with good experience and get their input. Synthesize the information until you come up with a personalized strategy that fits your abilities. So, what could the officers have done better in the Rodney King situation? What could have been done in the Beverly Hills Bank Robbery situation?

3) *Handcuff and then search.* There is no position of tactical advantage that is as good as having a suspect handcuffed. As soon as the determination to arrest has been made, use strong verbal commands to get the suspect in handcuff position and handcuff the suspect behind his back. A thorough search is safer with the suspect handcuffed.

4) *Use strong, simple verbal commands to gain compliance.* Strong verbal commands are the officer's best weapon. They allow the officer to articulate important information while maintaining a safe, tactical distance. If the suspect is complying, use commands to get him into a position of disadvantage (for handcuffing, this is on the knees, sitting back on the ankles, wrists touching behind the back). If compliance is not forthcoming, the officer can consider this heightened threat from a safe distance.

5) *Travel light.* Officers, especially newer officers, feel it is necessary to carry every piece of equipment offered in every catalogue. The officer becomes so weighed down with equipment that will never be used that he can barely move. An officer needs his weapon, an extra magazine, a less than lethal option to the weapon, a portable radio, handcuffs, flashlight and latex gloves. Any other objects are unnecessary and will only serve to encumber an officer.

An officer does not need a huge briefcase in the front seat, either. Placing a briefcase in the front passenger seat only takes away a possible route of tactical retreat for an officer. What paperwork does an officer need *immediate* access to? The patrol chart, a summons book and a warning book. All other reports, paperwork, pens, templates, protein bars and literature should be stored in the trunk and accessed when needed. The unit is not an officer's office; it is his sanctuary during time of attack—make sure it is accessible.

6) *Stop only one vehicle at a time.* An officer and his backup can only safely investigate one vehicle at a time. Even if there are multiple offenders, stop only one vehicle. Do not stop another vehicle until the first one has left the scene.

Stopping more then one vehicle creates a difficult situation for an officer. It also subjects unwary violators to the unknown risk created by the presence of the other violator.

7) *There are no "Routine Motor Vehicle Stops."* There are routine motor vehicle offenses and making motor vehicle stops may become a routine part of an officer's job but there are no routine stops. An operator getting stopped believes he is getting stopped for the worst thing he has ever done—that is to say, an officer may see an operator without a seatbelt and decide to conduct a "routine" stop. The vehicle operator knows he just robbed a bank and is sure that the officer is coming to apprehend him for this felony. The vehicle operator is in "felony fight mode," whereas an unprepared officer is in "routine stop, one-more-ticket-before-coffee mode." Treat every stop and approach every vehicle with the utmost of caution.

REALITY CHECK

DEADLY TRAFFIC STOP IN ILLINOIS REMINDS US TO ASSESS ALL STOPS AS RISKS

By Kisty Hoffman, Newsline Editor, Calibre Press Street Survival
Reprinted with the permission of Calibre Press
(www.calibrepress.com)

Late Saturday night Dimas Santiago, 63, observed the flashing lights in his rearview mirror after he made an illegal turn at Route 25 and the State Street intersection in Geneva, Ill. He knew what he had done wrong as he pulled into The Pride of Geneva Citgo gas station, and he probably began to panic and grow angry as he recalled all the trouble he'd already been in with the cops. He had been sentenced to 16 years in the pen in the late 1970s for attempted murder, and then several less serious scrapes with the law, including driving under the influence, in the 80s and 90s.

While all this may have been occurring to Santiago, the Geneva police officer conducting this traffic stop had no idea that the individual he was about to encounter had a history of criminality and a disrespect for law enforcement. For all he knew, Santiago was just an older gentleman who committed a minor traffic violation – what would seem to some people like no big deal.

But unfortunately, it was a big deal. The 29-year-old officer (a six-year veteran whose name is not being released at this time) approached the driver's side door to ask Santiago for his license and insurance information, and Santiago stepped out of the car wielding a "kitchen knife," with a serrated edge, at the officer, Geneva Police Lt. Joe Frega told news reporters.

The officer ordered Santiago to stop, but he resisted, so the officer fired off two rounds striking Santiago in the chest.

Santiago died at 12:07 am Sunday at Delnor-Community Hospital.

CHAPTER 7

Written Exercises

Traffic Stop Location Selection Exercise

Directions: The officer should become familiar with the map provided. Based on each situation presented, determine the best location to conduct the motor vehicle stop.

1) Friday, 7PM. A vehicle traveling south on 4th St. disregards the red light at Broadway.

2) A man with an active warrant is traveling west on Broadway crossing 1st Street. He has been arrested in the past and usually puts up a minor physical struggle.

3) Friday 6PM. A vehicle wanted in connection with an armed bank robbery is observed traveling west on Avenue A crossing 1st Street. (assume backup officers are 20 seconds away).

4) Sunday 10AM. A vehicle traveling east on Broadway disregards the red light at Main Street.

5) Friday 3PM. A vehicle traveling east on Avenue A disregards the red light at 5th Street.

6) Saturday 3PM. A vehicle traveling east on Avenue A disregards the red light at 5th Street.

7) Saturday 3PM. A vehicle traveling south on Main Street disregards the red light at Avenue B then turns right onto Avenue C.

8) Tuesday, midnight. A vehicle traveling north on 2nd Street ignores a red light and turns left onto Broadway.

9) Friday, 1PM. Vehicle traveling west on Avenue B disregards the red light at 1st Street.

10) Wednesday, noon. A vehicle with a cracked windshield is traveling east on Avenue B and turns right onto Main Street.

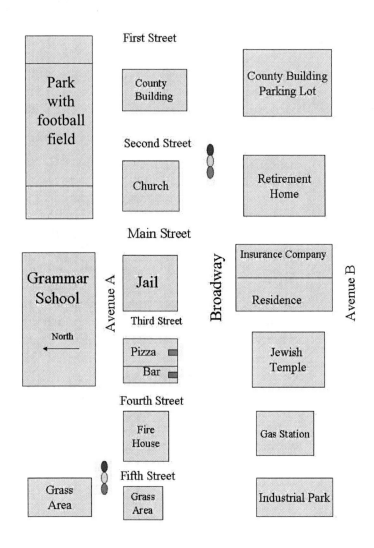

Discussion for Traffic Stop Location Selection Exercise

Situation #1. The officer should conduct the stop on 4th Street between Avenue B and Avenue C. The Temple between Broadway and Avenue B will be very crowded on a Friday night at 7PM. If the stop crosses Avenue C, it would be conducted in a radio dead zone next to fast food restaurant that is apt to be crowded on a Friday night. Between Avenue B and Avenue C there is a bank and a post office both of which would be closed on Friday night.

Situation #2. The stop should be conducted on Broadway between Main Street and 3rd Street, next to the jail. This is not really a high-risk stop. The minor physical resistance met in the past would not require the use of a firearm; more likely physical force would be used to subdue the offender. The jail has many officers working who could provide immediate assistance in a physical confrontation.

Situation #3. This is a high-risk stop and should be conducted in as isolated an area as possible. Most of downtown would be congested with rush hour traffic so this stop should be conducted on Avenue A, west of 5th Street, adjacent to the grassy area near the industrial park. By 6 pm on Friday night the industrial park should be rather empty.

Situation #4. The stop should be conducted on Broadway between 2nd Street and 1st Street. On Sunday morning, it is a reasonable assumption the church will be clogged with vehicular and pedestrian traffic. The County building is a Monday-Friday, 9 am to 5 pm operation which should be vacant and provide the officer with a safe area to conduct the stop.

Situation #5. This stop should be conducted on Avenue A between Main Street and 2nd Street. Anywhere on

Avenue A west of Main Street will be busy with children getting out of school. Avenue A at 2nd Street is near a church (which should be empty) and a park which should be somewhat vacant on a weekday afternoon.

Situation #6. This stop should be conducted on Avenue A at 4th Street. The school should be empty on a Saturday afternoon and the firehouse is a police friendly location.

Situation #7. This stop should be conducted on Avenue C on the industrial park side of 5th Street. Anywhere else, the officer is in a radio dead zone, police hostile location and/or on a bridge (no shoulder, possible discarding of evidence).

Situation #8. This stop should be conducted on Broadway between 4th Street and 5th Street. At the late hour, the officer will want the light provided by the gas station and the presence of the firefighters. The roadway also widens providing a safer approach and more room for passing traffic.

Situation #9. This stop should be conducted on Avenue B between Main Street and 3rd Street. The Mosque will be crowded on Friday at 1PM (the time of weekly Islamic religious ceremony) and the Lunch Time Café will also be crowded. The area next to the insurance company and Knights of Columbus should not be very crowded. Avoid the bank, which is commonly crowded on a Friday.

Situation #10. This stop has to be conducted almost immediately in front of the Knights of Columbus. Otherwise the officer is conducting a stop for a very minor traffic offense in a police hostile location and a radio dead zone.

Discretion Exercise

Directions: The officer should determine what law enforcement action is appropriate based on the facts presented. Options include issuing a summons, issuing a written warning, issuing a verbal warning and ignoring the offense.

1) A school bus full of nuns is double-parked in front of an orphanage as the nuns deliver medical supplies to the orphans.
2) Across from police headquarters you observe a civilian vehicle parked in a spot marked "Reserved for Police Vehicles Only."
3) On July 4, at 7:00PM, you observe a vehicle "doing donuts" in the Dairy Queen parking lot.
4) At 2:00AM while on routine patrol on the last night of the World Cup soccer tournament between Italy and Mexico, you observe approximately 20 cars double-parked on the dead end street next to San Remo's Sons of Sicily Bar and Athletic Club.
5) You stop your mother for traveling 45 MPH in a 25 MPH zone.
6) You stop your ex-wife for traveling 45 MPH in a 25 MPH zone.
7) You stop a college student for traveling 45 MPH in a 25 MPH zone.
8) You stop an off-duty police officer for traveling 45 MPH in a 25 MPH zone.
9) On July 15, you stop your town's biggest high school football star (who has a scholarship to Penn State) for a broken taillight and you find a very small amount of marijuana.
10) At 2AM, two white males drive into drug-infested housing projects from the north side entrance. At 2:02AM the same two white males are observed driving out of the south side exit of the projects.

Discussion for Discretion Exercise

In most of the cases, there are no "correct" answers. Discretion takes on many forms. Responses will not match even with officers from the same department, with the same training. Each situation does require addressing some of the facts presented before deciding what enforcement action to take.

Situation #1: If the nuns are not causing a major traffic tie-up and seem to be moving along swiftly, a verbal warning should suffice.

Situation #2: The officer's response will be dictated by the presence of a law on the books pertaining to this offense. Has this law been enacted (duly promulgated)? If so, the officer would want to consider the inconvenience being caused by the offense and weigh it against the business the offending driver is conducting (is the driver there to pick up the fatal accident report which killed his son?).

Situation #3: Date and time affect this enforcement. It can be assumed that on a hot summer night an ice cream shop will be crowded with patrons of all ages. If this is the case, this is a very dangerous offense and a summons should be issued.

Situation #4: In this era of community policing, officers must be aware of cultural differences in the community. In patrolling the area around the San Remo's Athletic Club and Bar it should be obvious to the officer that the World Cup final involving Italy would be of extra interest to this segment of the citizenry. Next, the officer should consider the location and time of day. It would seem unreasonable that at 2:00AM on a dead end street the double-parked vehicles are affecting the safe flow of traffic. Also, the officer should consider how the call was received? Are outraged citizens calling the police department demanding action? Are city officials holding meetings concerning this issue? Has this been an on-going problem? Finally, the officer should consider the possible response to the enforcement action.

Situation #4 falls under the category of "no enforcement action—the negative may outweigh the positive." The larger issue is that an officer must familiarize himself with his community and take steps to foster good relations within that community, even if it means disregarding some minor traffic offenses. Other common situations where issuing summons can do more harm than good:

- Funerals
- Large parties
- Days of Ethnic Pride and Celebration

In light of this situation the officer may want to contact other officers on duty and advise them that the quiet, 20-stool bar on the dead end street is unusually packed with people with the soccer game winding down and bar closing time arriving. No officer should ride to any job in that area alone.

Situation #5: In absence of serious bodily injury or death, a circumstance cannot be imagined when issuing one's mother a motor vehicle summons is the appropriate law enforcement action.

Situation #6: If the officer issues this summons, the headline in the paper the next morning is going to look pretty silly. She's probably put up with enough; let this one slide.

Situation #7: There are several types of college students. There are 19-year-olds who have never worked a day in their lives, driving dad's late model convertible. When stopped, the radio is not lowered and the cell phone conversation is not discontinued.

Then there is the single mom of 2, driving a 12-year-old vehicle, who is coming from her day job, trying to get to class because she knows it's the only way to improve her life and the lives of her children.

Situation #8: See Situation #5.

Situation #9: The officer should recognize at least two schools of thought in this situation:

Number 1: As a star high school athlete, this young adult has lived a life of entitlement. The school, the teachers, and the community have bent over backwards to accommodate this super-star. It is about time he learns he has to be responsible for his actions. He may have gotten away with violating the rules in high school but high school is now officially over.

Number 2: This student-athlete has the chance of a lifetime. An expensive education and possibly a million dollar career lay ahead. Should that all be taken away because of a small amount of marijuana, an immature mistake that many people his age make? The officer has to realize this may be a very expensive summons and arrest.

Situation #10: No legal enforcement action may be taken. Review **Reasons to Stop a Vehicle.** None of the criteria are met. The officer observed no actions that would lead a reasonable person to believe a crime has been committed. If the vehicle is stopped based on assumed criminal behavior, that would constitute racial profiling.

General Knowledge Exercise   (Answer Key: Page 162)

Directions: Using the officer's jurisdictional Criminal Code and the text, answer the following questions:

1) In the officer's jurisdiction, what is the criminal code for eluding?

2) In the officer's jurisdiction, what is the criminal code for providing false information (a false name, date of birth, social security #, etc.) to an officer?

3) In the officer's jurisdiction, what is the criminal code for refusing to produce required paperwork?

4) Define "discretion."

5) What is one example of "good discretion?"

6) What is one example of "bad discretion?"

7) On a motor vehicle stop, when is the threat over?

8) What Supreme Court decision governs when a motor vehicle can be stopped?

9) What Supreme Court decision governs when a driver can be removed?

10) What Supreme Court decision governs when a passenger can be removed?

11) What is the most common cause of injury to an officer on a motor vehicle stop?

12) What three special threats do motorcycles and their operators present?

13) Besides a motor vehicle violation, what is a lawful reason to stop a motor vehicle?

14) Name an attribute of a good location to conduct a motor vehicle stop.

15) Name an attribute of a bad location to conduct a motor vehicle stop.

16) Name a "police friendly" location.

17) Name a "police hostile" location.

18) Name a factor that would make a stop a "high-risk" stop.

19) Ascribing criminal conduct to a person based on their race is called _____.

20) Not taking law enforcement action based on allegiance to a race, nationality, ethnic group, etc. is called _____.

21) What is the statute of limitations on an equipment violation?

22) What is the statute of limitations on a moving violation?

23) What is the overriding priority for an officer in every situation?

Answer Key: Page 162

Picture Test

Directions: Officers are presented with photos of motor vehicle stops in progress. They are to note what the officers are doing wrong in each picture.

Picture 1:

Picture 2:

Picture 3:

Picture 4:

Picture 5:

Picture 6:

Picture 7:

Picture 8:

Picture 9:

Picture 10:

Picture 11:

Picture 12:

Picture 13:

Picture 14:

Picture 15:

Picture Test–Discussion

Picture 1 — Officer is shown leaning into offending vehicle, across a front passenger to retrieve paperwork. The officer should never lean into the vehicle. The credentials should be handed out to the officer. As the officer leans in he loses balance and is susceptible to being pulled into the vehicle.

Picture 2 — Officers are poorly positioned and have created a cross-fire. Officers should be at a right angle to each other, forming the letter "L" with the suspect.

Picture 3 — Officer is writing a summons with his window up and head down. Officer is unaware of citizen standing at his window.

Picture 4 — Officer has his gun drawn on a suspect as his partner is attempting to physically restrain the suspect. The officer's weapon should be holstered and he should be assisting his partner.

Picture 5 — Officer approaches offending vehicle with a portable radio in his weapon hand and a summons book in his support hand. Weapon hand must always remain empty.

Picture 6 — Officer is interviewing vehicle operator out of the vehicle with his back to the front passenger.

Picture 7 — Officer has approached on driver's side. He is bending over, speaking to the operator with his rear end very close to passing traffic. He is leaning forward, off balance and is resting on the offending vehicle.

Picture 8 — Officer is standing too close to suspect collecting information on a note pad. The officer should be at least 3 feet away, not directly in front of the suspect, with a physical barrier (such as the vehicle trunk) between him and the suspect. The suspect should be doing the writing so his hands are encumbered. The officer can watch and ask questions from a safe distance.

Picture 9 — Officer is conducting the stop from the driver's side. The driver is turning his body in such a way that the officer can not see the vehicle interior.

Picture 10 — Officer in unit, writing summons, with a huge briefcase next to him, a bag of fast food near him, newspapers on the dashboard, cold drink in his hand, smoking a cigar, on a cell phone, etc. An officer must concentrate all his efforts on writing the summons quickly and observing the vehicle occupants.

Picture 11 — Officer is searching the trunk with occupants standing behind him.

Picture 12 — Officer being confronted by a suspect with a knife (deadly force) and does not have his weapon drawn.

Picture 13 — An officer is conducting a stop while his partner is on the sidewalk distracted by looking at a map and giving directions to another motorist.

Picture 14 — Officer removing driver's license from a female's wallet. Officer is poorly positioned on the driver's side, in the roadway. Both hands are encumbered with the task of removing the driver's license from the wallet. The officer has almost turned his back on the vehicle operator.

Picture 15 — Officer is conducting a search under the driver's seat from a bad position. He is blindly reaching into an area he cannot see. An officer must get in proper position to visually observe a location before putting his hand there. This will avoid the nasty surprise of open-edged weapons, exposed syringes, jagged metal, etc.

CHAPTER 8

Practical Exercises

Preparation

In order to efficiently conduct the practical exercises, the training unit should have:

1) A first aid kit
2) A phone or radio that can be used to contact an ambulance, if necessary
3) A whistle (to stop the scenario)
4) A handcuff key
5) Inert chemical agent dispenser or a bottle that will simulate chemical agent during the training
6) Three (3) ziplock bags with approximately 5, 10 and 15 grams of oregano
7) Three (3) ziplock bags with approximately 5, 10 and 15 grams of baking soda
8) Three handguns that have been made inoperable.
9) A rubber training knife
10) Empty beer cans
11) Ace bandages (for the instructors' wrists, so when they get repeatedly handcuffed they do not sustain injury)
12) Pertinent paperwork (a driver's license, registration and insurance card)
13) One suspect vehicle
14) Two marked units
15) Two way radio communication
16) 8½" x 11" white paper, a black magic marker and scotch tape. Items used by the instructor to change the vehicle license plate for each scenario, giving each officer practice with the phonetic alphabet.
17) Incense sticks that, when burnt, emanate an odor of burnt marijuana (and matches). (If the

incense sticks are not available, the words "odor of burnt marijuana present" can be written on paper and taped to the window.)

18) Two (2) ballistic vests. One for the officer in training and another for the backup officer

19) Daily newspaper (to create clutter in vehicle and help obscure contraband)

20) Flashlights (to simulate night time stops)

Each officer in training should have:

1) a full duty belt with an unloaded weapon but no baton, live rounds or chemical agent
2) a flashlight
3) a memo pad
4) a pen
5) handcuffs and a handcuff key

General Ground Rules

1) NO LOADED WEAPONS ANYWHERE IN THE TRAINING AREA

2) NO LIVE AMMUNITION ANYWHERE IN THE TRAINING AREA

The training area should be cordoned off with crime scene tape. A safety officer should be assigned to check ANYONE coming to the training area to make sure no loaded weapons or live ammunition are present.

3) No one gets hurt. The instructors should emphasize that at no time will any officer be struck. The only force needed in these exercises is the minimal force needed to handcuff a compliant suspect. No scenario requires strikes or physical force of any type.

4) The officers must use the two-way radios provided and call in all stops.

5) The officer should always keep his weapon hand free.

6) The officer should articulate all communications in a professional manner. Radio communication should be brief and efficient. Conversation with vehicle occupants should be professional. When articulating the reason for the stop, do not use colloquial language, meaning:

- An operator disregards a stop sign; he does not "blow a stop sign"
- An operator makes an improper u-turn; he does not "cut a u-ee in the middle of the street"
- An operator is traveling 40 mph in a 25 mph zone; he isn't "gunning it down da road"

All offenders are referred to as "Sir" and "Ma'am" no matter how they are treating the officer.

Language should be closely monitored. Absolutely no swearing or unprofessional verbiage can be tolerated. Remember, act as if everything is being videotaped.

7) Present the information in a manner that allows the officer being trained to come to a conclusion himself.

8) Do not stop the scenarios unless there is an injury. Make the officer work through the problem. Giving up and turning to an instructor is not an option on the street and should not be an option in training. That being said, there must be a safety code word in place that, if spoken by the officer or a training officer, indicates the scenario is immediately over. Things will get hot during this training and if a situation is getting out of hand, any of the

participants can immediately halt the training. The safety code can be any word as long as all participants know it ("safety break" has always worked well).

9)   Encourage the officer to use distance and time. These are two "friendly factors" that are always present to an officer. Distance creates safety and also creates time to think. If an officer is stuck or feels danger is present, create distance and clearly think of the next tactical step.

10)   Encourage the officers to gain compliance through strong verbal commands. This will help maintain distance. Do not approach a suspect until he is in a position of disadvantage. The verbal commands negate any reason for an officer to have to be within 10 feet of a suspect until that suspect is in a position of disadvantage.

11)   Anything less then getting killed earns praise for the officer. Priority #1 of this training is officer safety. If the officer has gone through the whole scenario and not been killed, he did a good job. There is no arrest, no load of drugs and no warrant arrest that is worth an officer's life. No one has ever died from missing a bag of drugs; officers have died in the reckless, unsafe pursuit of a bag of drugs. Safety and survival are the goal of every stop and every tour of duty.

Physical Layout of Practical Exercises

1)   The area where training is to be conducted should be cordoned off by cones, crime scene tape, barricades or some other physical barrier.

2)   A good training class should have 10-15 officers being trained with at least 4 instructors. One instructor must be the lead instructor. A

different instructor should be designated safety instructor; he is in charge of checking all weapons.

3) Ideally, the instructors should be able to prepare for each stop with the primary officer and backup officer out of sight.

4) 2 officers receive instruction at a time. The backup officer is not used in many of the scenes. He remains out of sight and becomes the primary officer in the next scene.

5) The officers not receiving training must remain silent and actively observe the stop. The officers not receiving training will be asked at the end of each scenario: "What went well?" "What did not go so well?" This encourages active watching and listening.

6) Each scenario should last 5-10 minutes with approximately the same amount of time dedicated to critique and discussion.

7) The instructors should conduct a stop to demonstrate the proper technique prior to any scenarios.

Scenarios

SCENARIO # 1	
Set up	Actor in the driver's seat, actor in the front passenger seat
Reason for stop	Speeding 40 mph/25 mph zone
Problem	Operator does not have a driver's license or any identification
Past officer's actions	The officer asks the operator questions in front of the passenger
Suggested action	Separate the occupants. Remove the operator from the front seat and place him on the hood, out of earshot from the passenger. Have him write his name and date of birth and any other pertinent information.
	Then interview the passenger to see if the information matches. If the information matches, it is reasonable to presume they are telling the truth. If the information does not match, it is likely they are lying.
	The officer should not allow the driver and passenger to discuss the answers.
	Check the officer's position when interviewing the driver. Is he maintaining a visual on the passenger? Is there a safe distance between him and the seated operator?
	Is the occupant directed into a position of disadvantage (elbows on knees, hands clasped together and with chin resting in hands) ?
	Have the operator print the information. It reduces the chance of miscommunication and keeps the operator's hands encumbered while the officer's hands are free. The writing is also proof in court of false information to the police.

SCENARIO # 2	
Set up	Actor in the driver's seat, actor in the front passenger seat
Reason for stop	Speeding 40 mph/25 mph zone
Problem	Upon being stopped, the driver runs off
Past officer's actions	The officer chases the driver. This leaves the passenger in a running vehicle.
Suggested action	Secure the scene. Take the keys and secure the passenger in the rear of the patrol car. Conduct an investigation. With the vehicle and a passenger, it is highly likely a safe apprehension will be made at a later date.
	Whether the officer patrols in an urban or rural setting, chasing a suspect is a low return risk. Officers are encumbered by heavy shoes, a ballistic vest and a duty belt. Catching a suspect is unlikely. The officer will be caught away from the unit in an unknown area. The unit is still running and may have other equipment (such as a shotgun) in it. The officer may be lured away from his unit and return to the scene without the suspect, missing his unit or its contents. Unless the officer is certain he can run down the suspect, chasing a non-felon is not recommended.

SCENARIO # 3	
Set up	Driver and front passenger
Reason for stop	Speeding 40 mph/25 mph zone
Problem	The vehicle is registered and insured. The operator is suspended. The passenger has valid driving privileges.
Past officer's actions	The officer tows the vehicle due to the suspended driver.
Suggested action	The vehicle is not in violation, the operator is. The vehicle can be operated by a valid driver–in this case, the passenger.

SCENARIO # 4	
Set up	Actor in the driver's seat, actor in the front passenger seat
Reason for stop	Speeding 40 mph/25 mph zone
Problem	Driver refuses to roll down window. With the radio turned up loud and the doors locked the occupants will not roll down the window. They act as if they cannot hear the officer or the window is broken. At some point the occupants hand pertinent paperwork out of the vehicle through a small crack in the window.
Past officer's actions	Pounding on the roof, yelling at the occupants.
Suggested action	The officer has a decision to make. He can lawfully order the driver out of the vehicle. If the driver refuses to comply, the situation has escalated from a motor vehicle stop to a criminal situation. If the driver is placed under arrest and still refuses to open the door, felony vehicle extraction techniques must be employed.

The courts have allowed officers to remove vehicle operators in absence of any reasonable suspicion of crime. The officers should use this privilege judiciously.

If the officer believes removing the driver will yield fruits of a crime, the officer should use all means available. If the officer feels the occupants are just being silly and are not really involved in criminal behavior, written enforcement action may suffice. |

SCENARIO # 5	
Set up	Vehicle operator in driver's seat
Reason for stop	Speeding 40 mph/25 mph zone
Problem	A small ziplock baggie (approx. 10 grams) of suspected marijuana is in plain view on the vehicle dashboard.
Past officer's actions	Officer reaches into vehicle to remove evidence. Officer conducts field interview about evidence without handcuffing the driver. Failure of officer to observe contraband.
Suggested action	Once the officer has probable cause to believe a crime has been committed, the operator should be placed under arrest, handcuffed behind the back, searched and advised of rights per Miranda.
	The officer does not want to reach into the vehicle without the suspect being secured or with the vehicle running. The officer must know to handcuff then search. There is no position the suspect can be placed in that is more safe then having him handcuffed behind his back. The search does not commence until the suspect is handcuffed behind his back. Once the suspect is handcuffed, the search of the body does not begin in the area that is most likely to reveal contraband but rather in the area most accessible to the suspect, that is to say, his lower back area.
	A proper suspect search has at least 2 stages, the back and front. To search the back side, the handcuffed suspect is placed with his forehead on the trunk of his vehicle with his feet back. To search the front side, the suspect is bent backwards at the waist over the trunk of his vehicle. A shrewd suspect will "help" the officer by pressing his belt buckle area against the vehicle during the search; all he is doing is making that area inaccessible to the officer's search.

There should be no rush on the part of the officer to secure the evidence. The evidence will neither hurt the officer nor flee. The evidence will be exactly where the officer left it. The suspect must be arrested, handcuffed and searched before securing evidence and conducting a vehicle search.

Review proper search techniques. Pockets are to be squeezed first to determine the presence of any items – do not allow officers to blindly stick their hands in unchecked pockets. The same applies to under car seats. The officer must get down and look under the seat with his flashlight – do not blindly feel around under a seat.

If the officer missed the marijuana, it is not the worst thing in the world. No officer has ever died due to missing a small bag of marijuana. The officer should be encouraged to check his body positioning on the stop. Once the operator is clear of any weapons and the pertinent paperwork has been secured, the officer should move from the doorjamb position to the front windshield position for a plain view search of the vehicle interior.

SCENARIO # 6	
Set up	Vehicle operator in driver's seat
Reason for stop	Speeding 40 mph/25 mph zone
Problem	Operator has an active traffic warrant for $1,000.00
Past officer's actions	Not treating a traffic warrant arrest as seriously as a criminal arrest. Lazy search techniques.
Suggested action	The officer should still use strong verbal commands and the search procedures listed above even when dealing with a "minor" crime.

SCENARIO # 7	
Set up	Vehicle operator in driver's seat
Reason for stop	Speeding 40 mph/25 mph zone
Problem	A gun in plain view sticking out from under passenger seat.
Past officer's actions	Failure to observe weapon. Failure to switch to "high-risk stop" mode.
Suggested action	The officer does not need to stare at the occupant during the entire stop. Once the operator is cleared of any weapons, the officer must conduct a plain view search of the vehicle interior. Unlike the marijuana in scenario # 4, officers may die if they do not observe weapons. Upon observing the weapon, the officer must take a tactical position (it is recommended to return to the patrol unit), call for backup, wait for backup then conduct a high-risk stop. Officers are often hesitant to switch to "high risk" mode but it is the only way to conduct the stop in the presence of weapons.

SCENARIO # 8	
Set up	Operator in driver's seat
Reason for stop	Speeding 40 mph/25 mph zone
Problem	Operator provides all paperwork but as officer returns to unit to write summons operator will not remain in vehicle.
Past officer's actions	Arguing with operator trying to get him to remain in his vehicle.
Suggested action	Direct the operator to stay in his vehicle. He is not lawfully obligated to do so. As long as he is not interfering with traffic or posing a safety threat to himself or others, he can remain outside his vehicle. The officer should back the unit up about 50 feet and pay extra attention to the subject as he writes the ticket.

SCENARIO # 9	
Set up	5 burly males in a vehicle
Reason for stop	Speeding 40 mph/25 mph zone
Problem	The occupants immediately exit the vehicle and approach the officer in a menacing and aggressive manner.
Past officer's actions	Officer engages the occupants in verbal confrontation. The officer attempts to subdue one of the occupants and winds up getting attacked by all of the occupants. The officer gets surrounded and separated from his unit.
Suggested action	The officer must be aware of his surroundings (where he is) and his resources (availability and proximity of backup). The officer must consider if backup is available and how long it will take them to get to his location. If the officer is obviously out-numbered and the occupants are approaching, this is at least a mechanical force situation and possibly a deadly force situation. The officer must honestly assess his desire to use deadly force. In some situations the offenders may be too close or on the officer too quickly for the officer to draw his weapon. If the stop cannot be safely conducted, the officer has to remove himself from the scene, and investigate the operator and his vehicle when resources are present that allow a safe investigation. Conducting the stop against impossible odds is only going to get the officer hurt. Unfortunately, the graveyard is full of cops who displayed "Tombstone Courage." This is a good chance to review the concept of the backup officer. The officer should be able to assess realistically how long it will take backup to respond. In training scenarios backup is right around the corner; on the street, this is often not the case.

SCENARIO # 10	
Set up	Driver and front passenger
Reason for stop	Speeding 40 mph/25 mph zone
Problem	Upon approach, a small baggie of marijuana is thrown out of the passenger window. It is impossible to tell whether the driver or occupant threw the baggie and neither admit to it.
Past officer's actions	Officer secures the evidence without securing the occupants. Officer conducts a long investigation/street trial at the scene attempting to extract a guilty plea from one of the occupants.
Suggested action	Once the officer has probable cause to believe the substance is illegal, attention must be turned to the occupants; specifically, they should be arrested, handcuffed, searched and advised of rights per Miranda. Spending time with the evidence is only allowing more time for unsecured, possibly armed suspects to be loose. With the occupants secured and searched, the officer can then field test the contraband and conduct whatever interrogation he wants. Only a judge can determine guilt or innocence. Offender admissions at the scene are of little importance and not much time should be spent trying to obtain them. This is a good scenario to review constructive possession assumptions.

SCENARIO # 11	
Set up	Driver and front passenger
Reason for stop	Speeding 40 mph/25 mph zone
Problem	A small baggie of marijuana is stealthily placed near the vehicle by a third person (not the vehicle occupants). Efforts must be made so the officer does not see who places the marijuana.
Past officer's actions	The officer sees the baggie of marijuana proximate to the vehicle and assumes a vehicle occupant discarded it. As with scenario # 8, both occupants deny it. The officer wrongly arrests both occupants. The occupants are cooperative but continue to express their innocence.
Suggested action	The scenario is stopped with both (cooperative) occupants handcuffed. Fast forward to the "trial" where the officer swears "to tell the truth, the whole truth and nothing but the truth." He "testifies" that the occupants were in possession of marijuana. This is obviously not true. The lessons are: 1. Act as if everything is videotaped. The officer must understand that the video tape from his unit, or taken by a civilian will expose the truth. 2. If You Did Not See It, It Did Not Happen!!! It is better to lose an arrest for a small amount of marijuana rather then lose credibility by lying about what was seen.

SCENARIO # 12	
Set up	Driver and front passenger
Reason for stop	Speeding 40 mph/25 mph zone
Problem	Upon approach, a large gun is discarded from the vehicle on the side opposite of the officer's approach.
Past officer's actions	The officer hears the sound but is uncertain about what it is, so he does nothing or, the officer does not hear the gun hit the ground.
Suggested action	If the officer locates the gun on the ground, he must immediately switch to "high risk" mode. Take cover back at the unit, call for backup and executes a high-risk stop.
	The high risk element of this scenario can be enhanced by having the search of an occupant reveal another weapon. Never assume that the contraband found is the only contraband present.
	If the officer does not hear the gun hit the ground, he must be encouraged to use all his senses at all times on motor vehicle stops.
	To create realism in the high-risk stop scenario, other officers originally not in the scenario may be dispatched to act as backup officers. The primary officer must control the scene.

SCENARIO # 13	
Set up	Driver and front passenger
Reason for stop	Speeding 40 mph/25 mph zone
Problem	Officer observes rolling papers in plain view.
Past officer's actions	Occupants are placed under arrest.
Suggested action	Rolling papers by themselves are legal. They can be bought in any convenience store. This situation would require follow-up questions and maybe a request to search but not an arrest.

SCENARIO # 14	
Set up	Operator in driver's seat. Operator has a gun in his waistband and on his ankle (or jacket pocket).
Reason for stop	Speeding 40 mph/25 mph zone
Problem	The driver has an active warrant for $1,000.00
Past officer's actions	The officer locates one weapon and stops his search. Officer does not properly secure located weapon during rest of suspect search.
Suggested action	The officer must be trained in thorough and complete searches. Searches incident to arrest are very intrusive in that the officer is looking for *any* contraband–not just weapons. The search should be systematic and cover the body. Do not end the search when one weapon is found. While maintaining control of the suspect, secure the weapon. Use proper search techniques as outlined in scenario # 4.

SCENARIO # 15	
Set up	Operator in driver's seat
Reason for stop	Speeding 40 mph/25 mph zone
Problem	The operator exits his vehicle with a gun to his own head, demanding the officer gives up his weapon or the operator will commit suicide.
Past officer's actions	Very few officers have given up their weapons but many have given up cover and concealment.
Suggested action	This is a high-risk stop situation. Call for an ambulance, backup and appropriate medical assistance. Attempt to calm the subject. Remain calm. But do all this from behind cover and concealment, weapon drawn. If the subject gets too close, treat him as a non-compliant suspect with a weapon.

SCENARIO # 16	
Set up	Operator in driver's seat
Reason for stop	Speeding 40 mph/25 mph zone
Problem	A small baggie of marijuana is in the ashtray. The operator makes every effort to conceal the vehicle interior from the officer by blocking it with his body. The operator torques his body, leans, twists and does whatever he can to keep the officer from seeing the vehicle interior.
Past officer's actions	The officer never gets to a position where he can see the interior.
Suggested action	The officer must (lawfully) control all aspects of the stop. In this case, the operator will not move his body to allow a plain view interior search. The officer is lawfully allowed to remove the driver (*Pennsylvania v. Mimms*, 1977) and conduct his plain view search. Once the marijuana is located, steps outlined in scenario #4 should be followed.

SCENARIO # 17	
Set up	Operator in driver's seat
Reason for stop	Speeding 40 mph/25 mph zone
Problem	The operator has an active warrant for $1,000.00. The operator has a large amount of marijuana protruding from a jacket pocket or the front of the waistband of his jeans. The operator also has a gun in the lower back area of his jeans.
Past officer's actions	The officer focuses on the marijuana and seizes it before handcuffing the suspect. The suspect aids in allowing the officer to retrieve the marijuana by placing his hands behind his back.
Suggested action	As outlined in scenario #4, upon probable cause of a crime or arrest, the suspect is to be immediately handcuffed. The search does not start with the contraband but rather the area accessible to the suspect.

SCENARIO # 18	
Set up	Two subjects are looking under the raised hood of a disabled vehicle. One of the subjects has a gun in his hand but his hands are resting on his hips and the officer can not see the gun.
Reason for stop	Dispatched to investigate a disabled motorist or during routine patrol the officer happens upon the situation.
Problem	The subject has a gun in his hand.
Past officer's actions	Due to the fact this is not a criminal contact or motor vehicle stop, the officer is not assertive in ordering the subject to show his hands. The scenario continues until the subject gets the tactical advantage on the officer and puts the gun to the officer's head.
Suggested action	The officer must be taught that all situations are potentially dangerous and all subjects must be approached with the utmost of caution.

SCENARIO # 19	
Set up	Operator in driver's seat
Reason for stop	Speeding 40 mph/25 mph zone
Problem	The operator refuses to produce any pertinent paperwork.
Past officer's actions	The officer explains, pleads and threatens but never acts.
Suggested action	The officer must "draw a line in the sand" and at some point, arrest this operator consistent with the obstruction of justice statutes in the jurisdiction.

SCENARIO # 20	
Set up	Operator in driver's seat
Reason for stop	Speeding 40 mph/25 mph zone, weaving, vehicle does not immediately stop.
Problem	The operator is unresponsive in the front seat. He is seated with his head back, eyes closed. He is not making any sounds and does not respond to the officer.
Past officer's actions	The officer shouts at the operator, yells at him, pounds on the car, shakes him, etc. with no response from the operator.
Suggested action	For this scenario to be successful, the actor playing the operator can not cough or groan or breathe deeply. The officer is not confronted with a motor vehicle situation–this is a medical "non-breather" situation. The officer successfully concludes this scenario when he activates the ABC's of life saving (airway, breathing, circulation) and begins first aid on this subject. At the very least the officer should clear the airway and check for a pulse. An ambulance should be summoned to the scene.
	Other steps that should be taken in this situation:
	1) the vehicle is turned off and the keys are removed.
	2) the operator is handcuffed. The handcuffs can be applied in the front but until the officer knows the entire situation the cuffs should remain on. Is this operator drunk? high on PCP? in anaphylactic shock? in diabetic shock? having an adverse reaction to food? The officer has no way of knowing and until he does know, it is best to have the subject handcuffed for his own safety and the safety of the officer.
	3) the operator is pat searched. Rescue personnel and the officer will be very close to this subject for a long period of time. A quick search for weapons is expected.
	Instructors should time this scenario from the officer's initial contact to the point he clears the airway. Recognize that brain damage sets in after only 4 minutes of no oxygen to the brain.

SCENARIO # 21	
Set up	Sunday morning, 10AM. Officer is seated in a crowded diner taking his meal break.
Reason for stop	n/a
Problem	A 10-year-old boy with a friend approach the officer presenting a soiled handgun to the officer. They immediately place it on the table and say they found it out back while they were playing.
Past officer's actions	The officer attempts to clear the weapon in the crowded diner. The officer conducts an interview with the children in the diner with the weapon present.

Suggested action	Immediately secure the weapon in the trunk of the unit. Do not attempt to clear the weapon. The weapon is unknown to the officer and may be rigged or booby trapped. The weapon should immediately be brought to an area away from innocent citizens.
	
	    As the officer is hurrying out of the diner ask the manager or cashier to stay with the children.
	    Call for a supervisor.
	    Have the children come out near the unit and begin to obtain information about their find.

SCENARIO # 22	
Set up	Driver and front passenger
Reason for stop	Speeding 40 mph/25 mph zone
Problem	Odor of burnt marijuana is emanating from the vehicle interior
Past officer's actions	Asking about the smell and requesting consent to search.
Suggested action	The odor of burnt marijuana is probable cause a crime has been committed. This is usually enough reason to search the vehicle for the source of the odor.

SCENARIO # 23	
Set up	Male operator with pregnant female in the passenger seat
Reason for stop	Speeding 60 mph/25 mph zone
Problem	The female is screaming, apparently ready to give birth. The operator is highly agitated and wants an escort to the hospital.
Past officer's actions	Escorted the operator to the hospital.
Suggested action	Do not escort a civilian in a civilian vehicle to the hospital. If that person crashes, he will blame you for facilitating his reckless driving that led to the wreck. The officer does not know the driving capabilities of the operator or the condition of the vehicle. Do not escort the vehicle. Either call an ambulance and have the ambulance drive the pregnant woman to the hospital or let the driver go with a warning and his promise to slow down.

SCENARIO # 24	
Set up	Driver and front passenger
Reason for stop	Vehicle is wanted in connection with an armed robbery that happened 15 minutes ago, 10 miles away.
Problem	
Past officer's actions	
Suggested action	Officer should immediately recognize this is a high-risk stop. Initiate high-risk stop tactics. Any other action is not suggested. Officer should be checked for 1) vehicle positioning 2) body positioning 3) strong, simple verbal commands 4) command of situation

Scenario # 25	
Set up	Operator in driver's seat
Reason for stop	Speeding 40 mph/25 mph zone
Problem	A police friendly passer-by stops to "assist" the officer. He wears camouflage pants, a police t-shirt and carries a scanner. He watches "Cops" every week and reads cop comic books. His favorite movie is SWAT. He knows the departmental codes and supplements them with a few he makes up on his own. He politely asks the officer if help is needed and the officer politely declines his offer. The passer-by then begins to berate the operator (who to this point has been quiet and cooperative). The passer-by continues to badger the operator with worse and worse dialogue.
Past officer's actions	Due to the fact the passer-by is police friendly and somewhat of a local character, the officer does not do enough to separate the passer-by from the scene.
Suggested action	The officer has to take a firm, unbiased stand. Citizen support is always welcome but it cannot be allowed to digress into a name-calling situation. The passer-by should be asked to leave (maybe twice), then ordered to leave and, if he continues to agitate the situation, he must be arrested.

Scenario # 26	
Set up	Operator in driver's seat
Reason for stop	Speeding 40 mph/25 mph zone
Problem	As officer is writing the ticket, operator gets out of his vehicle to talk on cell phone.
Past officer's actions	Officer demands operator remains in vehicle.
Suggested action	The operator is under no legal obligation to remain in the vehicle.

SCENARIO # 27	
Set up	Operator in the driver's seat
Reason for stop	Speeding 40 mph/25 mph zone
Problem	The operator is verbally combative throughout the stop but provides required paperwork. When the summons is issued the operator refuses to take possession of it.
Past officer's actions	The officer argues with the operator to accept the summons.
Suggested action	In the absence of a law in the jurisdiction, the officer has to make a reasonable effort to serve the summons. If the operator refuses to receive the summons the officer should verbally advise a motor vehicle summons has been issued and place the summons and pertinent paperwork on the windshield, under the wipers, like a parking ticket.

SCENARIO # 28	
Set up	Operator in driver's seat
Reason for stop	Speeding 40 mph/25 mph zone
Problem	The operator states he is an off-duty police officer
Past officer's actions	The officer immediately lowers his guard.
Suggested action	Remain vigilant. Ask the operator if he has a weapon and if he does, where it is. Ask to see a badge **and** photo identification. If other officer's are known from that jurisdiction, check familiarity by asking simple, friendly questions. Ask questions that only police officers would know the answers to (specific motor vehicle statutes, specific criminal statutes etc.).

SCENARIO # 29	
Set up	Driver and front passenger
Reason for stop	Speeding 40 mph/25 mph zone
Problem	Operator is boisterous and verbally abusive to officer. Passenger is condescending and mocking toward officer. There is no physical contact or threat but the occupants are extremely nasty. After about 90 seconds of abuse, a citizen passes by and advises the officer there is a fire at the hospital 2 blocks away. The abuse continues and becomes worse. About 20 seconds later, another citizen advises of the fire. The abuse becomes louder and more nasty.
Past officer's actions	The officer continues to interact with the vehicle occupants.
Suggested action	Protecting human life is the overriding priority at all times. The officer must recognize that lives are in danger and respond to the hospital. Despite the fact the officer is anxious to take enforcement action against these abusive subjects, he must be professional enough to realize the importance of his response to the fire scene. Even if he gets to the hospital and realizes he was duped, it is better to err on the side of caution.

SCENARIO # 30	
Set up	Operator in driver's seat, front passenger
Reason for stop	Speeding 40 mph/25 mph zone
Problem	Initially, vehicle occupants are compliant. When officer returns to suspect vehicle to serve summons, one occupant is holding a handgun under his leg.
Past officer's actions	The officer does not re-approach the vehicle with the same level of caution as the initial approach.
Suggested action	The officer must be trained to maintain a high level of caution and the threat is not over until the offender re-enters traffic.

Scenario # 31	
Set up	Driver and front passenger
Reason for stop	Vehicle is wanted in connection with an armed robbery that happened 15 minutes ago, approximately 10 miles away.
Problem	The officer should recognize this is a high-risk stop and initiate high-risk stop tactics. After backup has arrived and the occupants have been removed one by one and placed face down on the pavement and handcuffed, communications advises they misunderstood the last character on the license plate. The vehicle stopped by the officer is not wanted in connection with the armed robbery—it is the vehicle owned by the mayor of the neighboring town.
Past officer's actions	The officer brings the occupants to the station for follow-up investigation.
Suggested action	The officer should un-cuff the mayor, apologize and send him on his way. The officer did not do anything wrong but he should still apologize for the inconvenience. The officer is expected to act only on the information he has at the time. He had reason to believe it was a high-risk stop and acted accordingly. Once more facts were known, he also acted accordingly.
	The mayor will be mad and may complain. But when he knows the facts, he will probably just let the issue go, knowing the officer did the right thing.
	A brief incident report covering what the officer heard and what he did may be completed by the officer in preparation for a phone call to internal affairs the next day.

SCENARIO # 32	
Set up	Operator in driver's seat
Reason for stop	Speeding 40 mph/25 mph zone
Problem	The operator is extremely upset. He is yelling, swearing and making very weak threats. He is throwing (non-hazardous) things (paper, plastic bottles, paper cups, magazines, etc.) out of the car (not at the officer). He does not stop the officer but rather rants on and on about various injustices and makes personal comments regarding the officer's appearance, profession, manhood, haircut, body type, his family, etc.
Past officer's actions	Standing there, trying to get the operator to calm down.

Suggested action	If there is no crime or probable cause of any crime, get on with writing the ticket. The operator can be as mad as he wants to be as long as the officer is not in danger. Issue the summons and serve it professionally.
	
	    The officer must exercise discipline. In the academy, discipline is taught by standing at attention, marching and other military related activities. This situation is the physical manifestation of discipline. The officer must rely on his training to remain calm, professional and safe. Do not be lured into verbal combat about personal appearance, etc.
	
	    The offender is not criticizing "John Smith," he is mad at Officer Smith of the Anytown Police Department. The comments should not be taken personally.
	
	    This is a good time to review "Operator responses to being stopped—Anger and Aggression." This is a case of anger.

SCENARIO # 33	
Set up	Operator in driver's seat
Reason for stop	Speeding 40 mph/25 mph zone
Problem	Operator has an active $1,000.00 warrant. Operator has a handcuff key taped into inside lower back area of jeans or taped behind belt in the back.
Past officer's actions	Officers search the suspect but miss the cuff key.
Suggested action	The officer must be systematic. The search incident to arrest is intrusive, looking for any type of contraband. The area most accessible to the suspect must be searched first.

SCENARIO # 34	
Set up	Operator in driver's seat
Reason for stop	Speeding 40 mph/25 mph zone
Problem	Operator has an active $1,000.00 warrant. Upon arrest, operator is extremely cooperative. At some point, the handcuffs become too tight on the suspect. Transport to headquarters is going to take about 30 minutes
Past officer's actions	Officer refuses to re-set the handcuffs.
Suggested action	Improperly applied handcuffs can be painful but can also cause serious bodily injury. If blood supply is cut off to a limb long enough, nerve damage may occur. The loss of a hand cannot be the penalty for a $1,000.00 warrant. The officer should check the handcuffs and readjust if necessary. This is best done with an assisting officer present. No matter what, the subject should be completely searched, then placed on his knees, ankles crossed, sitting back on his ankles prior to the handcuffs being removed.

SCENARIO # 35	
Set up	Operator in driver's seat
Reason for stop	Speeding 40 mph/25 mph zone
Problem	Operator has an active $1,000.00 warrant. Operator has a baggie of marijuana (or glassines of heroin, or a razor blade) inside of his baseball cap.
Past officer's actions	Officers search the suspect but miss the contraband.
Suggested action	The officer must be systematic. The search incident to arrest is intrusive, looking for any type of contraband. The area most accessible to the suspect must be searched first but all areas must be covered.

SCENARIO # 36	
Set up	Operator in driver's seat
Reason for stop	Speeding 40 mph/25 mph zone
Problem	The license plate called in does not match the make or model of the vehicle
Past officer's actions	Asking the operator about the violation.
Suggested action	The officer should compare the Vehicle Identification Number (VIN) on the vehicle to the VIN on file.
	The officer should have communications check the VIN for stolen as well as the fictitious plates.
	Officers should have a basic working knowledge of VINs and know where they are on the vehicle for cross reference purposes. Most jurisdictions have criminal statutes for defaced VINs; officers should be aware of this offense.

SCENARIO # 37	
Set up	Operator in driver's seat
Reason for stop	Speeding 40 mph/25 mph zone
Problem	Operator has an active $1,000.00 warrant. As the arrest is being made, communications keeps calling the officer advising of different warrants from different venues.
Past officer's actions	Officer stops the arrest process and answers the radio.
Suggested action	Ignore the radio and get the suspect handcuffed and searched. Whether the suspect has one warrant or one hundred warrants he will still have to be handcuffed and searched. Communications are certain they are helping by providing more information but they are actually hindering the officer. If the officer continues to stop the arrest procedure to answer the radio he is subjecting himself to physical danger from the suspect.

SCENARIO # 38	
Set up	Operator in driver's seat with a front passenger
Reason for stop	Speeding 40 mph/25 mph zone
Problem	Occupants refuse to show their hands. After 2 or 3 verbal directions the occupants put their hands on the dashboard. The passenger does not open one hand completely but rather holds a small bag of marijuana with one of his fingers.
Past officer's actions	Officer sees the occupants' hands but not the contents of the hands.
Suggested action	The officer must be careful and thorough. The officer does not just want to see the subject's hands, he wants to see the inside of the subject's hands.

SCENARIO # 39	
Set up	Male operator in driver's seat with female front passenger
Reason for stop	Speeding 40 mph/25 mph zone
Problem	Female is highly upset and crying. Male is angry and yelling. The operator produces required paperwork. The operator does all he can to reassure the officer everything is fine. The operator does not want the officer to talk to the female.
Past officer's actions	The officer takes the operator's word for things and does not interview the female.
Suggested action	The officer must conduct a complete investigation. The occupants must be interviewed separately. If any violence is reported or is manifested, appropriate arrest actions must be taken. Someone should observe the officer to make sure he can monitor one occupant while interviewing the other occupant.

SCENARIO # 40	
Set up	Operator in driver's seat with a front passenger.
Reason for stop	Speeding 40 mph/25 mph zone
Problem	Officer has conducted the stop in a "police hostile" location. A boom box blasts music from the sidewalk. Pedestrians are approaching the officer and the vehicle from all angles. Uninvolved citizens are attempting to engage the officer in conversation. Pedestrians are interacting with the vehicle occupants. The scene is very noisy. A (plastic) bottle is thrown. Firecrackers are set off...
Past officer's actions	The officer attempts to control the scene.
Suggested action	The officer is spread too thin and there are too many threats and distractions for one officer to handle. This is a very dangerous location to be investigating a very minor offense. A quick verbal warning and prompt exit are in order.

SCENARIO # 41	
Set up	Operator in driver's seat
Reason for stop	Speeding 40 mph/25 mph zone
Problem	Operator hands the officer pertinent paperwork and a $50 bill. When the officer attempts to return it, the operator does not take it, stating "that's not mine." The implication is the $50 now belongs to the officer.
Past officer's actions	The officer goes back to the unit to call a supervisor.
Suggested action	The officer should immediately return the $50 to the operator. This should be a two-step process; an offer, then an ultimatum. **Officer:** "Sir, here is the money you accidentally handed me." **Operator:** "That's not mine, it must be yours." **Officer:** "Sir, it is not mine, it is yours. And if you do not take it back I will assume it is a bribe. Bribery is a crime for which you will be immediately arrested. Do you want your $50 back or should I arrest you and keep it for evidence?"

SCENARIO # 42	
Set up	Operator in driver's seat
Reason for stop	Speeding 40 mph/25 mph zone
Problem	Upon approach to vehicle, officer observes several empty alcoholic beverage containers in plain view.
Past officer's actions	The officer does not conduct any impaired driver tests.
Suggested action	The officer should have a pre-plan as to how to handle impaired drivers. What questions will be asked and what psychophysical tests will be conducted. Officer should be careful to take special care with an impaired driver, especially near passing traffic.

SCENARIO # 43	
Set up	Operator in driver's seat
Reason for stop	Speeding 40 mph/25 mph zone
Problem	Operator has no identification but claims to have an in-state driver's license.
Past officer's actions	Officer takes the name and runs it without any type of cross check of information.
Suggested action	The officer must conduct an investigation. The operator can easily be giving a false name. Have the operator print his name, date of birth and social security number then sign the page (see scenario #1). The officer should have some questions ready to test the veracity of the subject's story. It is easy to know and use a brother's name and date of birth and say the social security number is unknown. But shouldn't the operator know how old he is? what sign of the zodiac he is? what year he graduated high school? a girlfriend's name and phone number? If a subject cannot answer these simple questions, he is probably lying.

SCENARIO # 44	
Set up	Operator in driver's seat
Reason for stop	Disregard of stop sign
Problem	A senior backup officer arrives and takes control of the scene. He makes inappropriate statements and uses too much force.
Past officer's actions	The officer does little or nothing to stop the senior officer.
Suggested action	The officer must be assertive. He must advise the senior man in no uncertain terms that it is his stop and those tactics will not be tolerated. There is a thin line between regaining control of a stop and embarrassing a senior man in public. The officer should clear this stop then meet with the senior man in private and straighten out any misunderstandings.
	This is another opportunity to speak on backup officers. When an officer calls for backup in a training setting, the backup is there promptly. In reality, backup is seldom closer then 5 minutes away. Also, the backup officer arriving may be a young, conditioned, intelligent officer or an out of shape, burnt out, cynical officer. Be certain to verbalize exactly what is expected of the backup officer. As a backup officer, swallow some pride and be prepared to do as you're told by the primary officer.

SCENARIO # 45	
Set up	An officer is lying between his unit and the suspect unit as backup turns the corner. The officer's weapon is missing and he seems to be unconscious. Upon seeing the backup unit arrive, (at least) 5 different civilians run 5 different ways. Two civilians begin providing confusing accounts of what occurred and descriptions of the actors. A man standing approximately 20 feet away is pointed out; he begins to run away.
Reason for stop	n/a
Problem	Officer has no idea what has occurred
Past officer's actions	Officer chases the "suspect." Officer conducts field interview.
Suggested action	The downed officer must be medically attended to and made safe. An ambulance, backup and a supervisor must be called. Witnesses can be held but not until every step is taken to address the medical condition of the injured officer.

SCENARIO # 46	
Set up	Operator in driver's seat, front passenger
Reason for stop	Speeding 40 mph/25 mph zone
Problem	The offenders immediately exit the vehicle and draw firearms on the officer. They order his hands up, then for him to relinquish his weapon.
Past officer's actions	The helplessness of the situation overwhelms him and he just gives up.
Suggested action	This is a horrible scenario to be caught in and even worse in real life. The officer must try to do something, anything, to protect his life. He has to talk, plead, pray, run, dive, roll, hide or anything else he can think of. Demise would seem inevitable but the officer must try to do something. He cannot just give up.

SCENARIO # 47	
Set up	Four occupants in the vehicle
Reason for stop	Speeding 40 mph/25 mph zone
Problem	All four occupants are in possession of marijuana (or they all have warrants). The officer must arrest four people but does not have that many sets of handcuffs.
Past officer's actions	Officer handcuffs two of the suspects and two remain unsecured.
Suggested action	The officer wants all persons secured somehow. One suspect's right wrist can be handcuffed to another's left wrist. This way, 2 sets of cuffs (which most officers carry) can be used to secure 4 persons. At least the suspects cannot run off. The suspects should be searched and seated with their backs against the passenger side of the patrol unit as the officer awaits backup. The officer should closely monitor these suspects until backup arrives and there are enough handcuffs to properly secure all suspects.

SCENARIO # 48	
Set up	Operator in driver's seat
Reason for stop	Speeding 40 mph/25 mph zone
Problem	Operator is irate over summons. He is going to make a complaint and take the officer to court. He wants a name and badge number.
Past officer's actions	The officer tries to mollify the operator. The officer gives a long speech about what he is trying to accomplish with traffic enforcement and why the operator should not be upset.
Suggested action	Politely and professionally give the operator a name, badge number, then the address and phone number of the court. Anything less or different makes it seem the officer is afraid of the subject's threats. If the officer has followed the procedures outlined in this book, he is a highly competent, trained professional—one who has nothing to fear.

So, there you have it. Theories, strategies, techniques, exercises and ideas culled from many years of street level police experience. To complete this book the authors supplemented their years of police experience and research by interviewing and discussing tactics with seasoned police officers, SWAT team members and law enforcement thinkers. Hopefully this text will inspire critical thinking and professional debate. It is the hope of the authors that this text continues the discussion on officer safety during motor vehicle stops and provides fodder for discussions which will further the profession. This is the last page of this text but hopefully this will not be the last word on safe motor vehicle enforcement.

Answer Key

1) Check local statutes
2) Check local statutes
3) Check local statutes
4) Discretion- exercise of judgment (p. 7)
5) Good Discretion- Severity of the offense etc. (p. 8-9)
6) Bad Discretion- Race, color, creed etc. (p. 10-15)
7) The threat is remains until the offender returns to traffic and departs the scene (p. 56)
8) Delaware v. Prouse (1979) (p. 16)
9) Pennsylvania v. Mimms (1977) (p. 60)
10) Maryland v. Wilson (1997) (p. 66)
11) Passing traffic cause the most injuries to officers on motor vehicle stops. (p. 33)
12) 1. Tools mounted within reach of operator
    2. Alterations to motorcycle may conceal weapons
    3. Motorcycle riders often wear clothing with extra pockets that may contain weapons or clothing thick enough to lessen the impact of a baton strike (p. 87-88)
13) Suspected criminal behavior (p. 16-17)
14) A straightaway with a broad shoulder (p. 19)
15) Active Driveway (p. 19)
16) A firehouse (p. 19)
17) Known gang hangouts (p. 19)
18) The vehicle or occupants have been involved in a felony offense (p. 71)
19) "racial profiling" (p. 11- 15)
20) Favoritism (p. 15)
21) Check local statutes
22) Check local statutes
23) Officer safety

Web sites to aid law enforcement officers to remain topical, maintain and upgrade their traffic enforcement skills.

http://www.calibrepress.com/
Calibre Press, a division of Primedia Workplace Learning, trains over 200,000 law enforcement officials annually. For over 20 years, Calibre has been the leader in law enforcement education, training and information, helping to save officers' lives while reducing officer and agency liability. Throughout widely recognized Street Survival Seminars, our mission is to provide the most informative and motivational survival training experience available to the law enforcement community. This unique seminar, developed and presented by the industry's leading trainers, is designed to help police personnel STAY SAFE and healthy throughout their careers regardless of assignment.

http://peace-officers.com/
This site has news and provides information on obtaining college degrees in criminal justice as well as employment information.

http://bjatraining.aspensys.com/
The BJA Law Enforcement Training Database is a catalog of all federally funded and supported training available to state and local law enforcement officials. Each database listing includes the training provider, a course description, eligibility criteria, and contact information.

http://www.copsonline.com
A site that has links to news, equipment and training.

**http://criminaljustice.state.ny.us/crimnet/ojsa/cjr/
finalg-a.htm**

This site is maintained by the New York State Division of Criminal Justice Services and provides governmental and legal links.

http://www.fletc.gov/index.htm

The homepage of the Federal Law Enforcement Training Center. This site will lead to some of the best law enforcement training in the world.

http://www.aslet.org/

The home page of the American Society of Law Enforcement Trainers.

http://www.policeintegritygroup.com/

The Police Integrity Group is a law-enforcement consulting and training company. They specialize in police integrity and accountability matters and help state and local law enforcement agencies maintain public legitimacy by proactively responding to potential community concerns.

http://www.ileeta.org/

The home page of The International Law Enforcement Educators and Trainers Association.

http://www.lawandordermag.com/

An on-line version of the magazine with training and employment information.

http://www.mctft.com/

Some of the best training available about motor vehicle stops and drug interdiction. They have e-courses and will also export training to your department.

http://www.counterdrug.org

This is some of the best training available in law enforcement. Comprehensive classes on a variety of topics.

http://www.policemag.com
The home page of Police magazine.

http://www.talkjustice.com/cybrary.asp
A web site with information on a wide variety of law enforcement topics

http://www.posai.org/
The Police Officers Safety Association offers free and low-cost training programs to law enforcement officers to increase their safety and effectiveness

http://www.refuseandresist.org/altindex
An anti-government/anti-police web site that encourages various forms of resistance. It is a good site to see what strategies protesters use and how they plan to disrupt public meetings.

http://www.thebackup.com/
A private company offering e-classes and classes on CD-ROM.

http://www.theiacp.org/
The home page of the International Association of Chiefs of Police. This excellent page has access to grant-funded training.

http://www.odmp.org/
The Officer Down Memorial Page. Honors officers who have deceased in the line of duty. Much can be learned studying the circumstances under which other officers have died.

References

Connor, G. Mitchell, D. & Standen, D. (2000). Vehicle Stops: Safety Strategies Tactical Procedures. Stipes Publishing LLC. Champaign, Illinois.

Government Accounting Office (2000). Racial Profiling: Limited data available on motorist stops. Washington, DC: US Government Accounting Office.

Harris, D. (1999, December). The stories, the statistics, and the law: Why "driving while Black" matters. Minnesota Law Review, 84, 265-326.

Lamberth, J.D. (1997). Report of John Lamberth, Ph.D. American Civil Liberties Union Web site: http://www.aclu.org/court/lamberth.html

Leonard, V. (1971). Police Traffic Control. Thomas Publishers. Springfield, Illinois.

National Highway Traffic Safety Administration (2000). Economic Impact of Motor Vehicle Crashes, 2000. Web site: http://www.nhtsa.dot.gov

New York Attorney General's Office (1999). The New York City Police Department's "stop and frisk" practices. New York: Author.

Office of the Attorney General (1999). Interim report of the state police review team regarding allegations of racial profiling. New Jersey: Author.

Petrocelli, M., Piquero, A., & Smith, M. (2003). Conflict theory and racial profiling: An empirical analysis of police traffic stop data. Journal of Criminal Justice, 31, 1 11.

Rayburn, M. (2002). Advanced Vehicle Stop Tactics. Looseleaf Law Publications, Inc. Flushing, New York.

San Diego, California Police Department (2000). Vehicle stop study: Mid-year report. San Diego, CA: Author.

San Jose, California Police Department (1999). Vehicle stop demographic study. San Jose, CA: Author.

Smith, M. & Petrocelli, M. (2001). Racial Profiling? A multivariate analysis of police traffic stop data. Police Quarterly, 4(1), 4-27.

Zingraff, M., Mason, M.H., Smith, W.R., Tomasokovic-Devey, D. (2000). Evaluating North Carolina State Highway Patrol data: Citations, warnings, and searches in 1998. North Carolina State University Web site: http://www.nccrimecontrol.org/shp/ncshp report.htm.

Index

NOTES

NOTES

NOTES

NOTES

Suicide by Cop
Practical Direction for Recognition,
Resolution and Recovery
by Vivian Lord

Police Management Examinations
by Larry Jetmore

Police Sergeant Examination Preparation Guide
by Larry Jetmore

Path of the Warrior
An Ethical Guide to Personal &
Professional Development in the Field
of Criminal Justice
by Larry F. Jetmore

The COMPSTAT Paradigm
Management Accountability in Policing,
Business and the Public Sector
by Vincent E. Henry, CPP, Ph.D.

The New Age of Police Supervision
and Management
A Behavioral Concept
by Michael A. Petrillo & Daniel R. DelBagno

Effective Police Leadership - 2nd Edition
Moving Beyond Management
by Thomas E. Baker, Lt. Col. MP USAR (Ret.)

The Lou Savelli Pocketguides -

Gangs Across America and Their Symbols
Identity Theft - Understanding and Investigation
Guide for the War on Terror
Basic Crime Scene Investigation